How to Use Your Reading in Your Essays

www.palgravestudyskills.com – the leading study skills website

Palgrave Study Skills

Business Degree Success
The Business Student's Phrase Book
Career Skills
Cite Them Right (10th edn)
Critical Thinking and Persuasive Writing for
  Postgraduates
e-Learning Skills (2nd edn)
The Employability Journal
Essentials of Essay Writing
Get Sorted
Great Ways to Learn Anatomy and Physiology
  (2nd edn)
How to Begin Studying English Literature (4th edn)
How to Study Foreign Languages
How to Study Linguistics (2nd edn)
How to Use Your Reading in Your Essays (3rd edn)
How to Write Better Essays (4th edn)
How to Write Your Undergraduate Dissertation
  (2nd edn)
Improve Your Grammar (2nd edn)
Information Skills
The International Student Handbook
The Mature Student's Guide to Writing (3rd edn)
The Mature Student's Handbook
Mindfulness for Students
The Palgrave Student Planner
The Personal Tutor's Handbook
Practical Criticism
Presentation Skills for Students (3rd edn)
The Principles of Writing in Psychology
Professional Writing (3rd edn)
Researching Online
The Student Phrase Book
The Student's Guide to Writing (3rd edn)
Study Skills for International Postgraduates
Studying in English
Studying History (4th edn)
Studying Law (4th edn)
Studying Modern Drama (2nd edn)
Studying Psychology (2nd edn)
Studying Physics
Success in Academic Writing (2nd edn)
Smart Thinking
The Undergraduate Research Handbook
The Work-Based Learning Student Handbook
  (2nd edn)
Work Placements – A Survival Guide for Students
Writing for Engineers (4th edn)
Writing History Essays (2nd edn)
Writing for Law
Writing for Nursing and Midwifery Students
  (2nd edn)
Write it Right (2nd edn)
Writing for Science Students

Pocket Study Skills

14 Days to Exam Success
Analyzing a Case Study
Blogs, Wikis, Podcasts and More
Brilliant Writing Tips for Students
Completing Your PhD
Doing Research (2nd edn)
Getting Critical (2nd edn)
Managing Stress
Planning Your Dissertation
Planning Your Essay (2nd edn)
Planning Your PhD
Posters and Presentations
Reading and Making Notes (2nd edn)
Referencing and Understanding Plagiarism
  (2nd edn)
Reflective Writing
Report Writing
Science Study Skills
Studying with Dyslexia (2nd edn)
Success in Groupwork
Time Management
Where's Your Argument?
Writing for University (2nd edn)

Palgrave Research Skills

Authoring a PhD
The Foundations of Research (2nd edn)
Getting to Grips with Doctoral Research
Getting Published
The Good Supervisor (2nd edn)
The Lean PhD
PhD by Published Work
The PhD Viva
The PhD Writing Handbook
Planning Your Postgraduate Research
The Postgraduate Research Handbook (2nd edn)
The Professional Doctorate
Structuring Your Research Thesis

Palgrave Career Skills

Excel at Graduate Interviews
Graduate CVs and Covering Letters
Graduate Entrepreneurship
How to Succeed at Assessment Centres
Social Media for Your Student and Graduate Job
  Search
The Graduate Career Guidebook
Work Experience, Placements and Internships

For a complete listing of all our titles in this area please visit **www.macmillanihe.com/study-skills**

HOW TO USE YOUR READING IN YOUR ESSAYS

Third Edition

Jeanne Godfrey

First edition 2009
Second edition 2013

This edition first published 2018 by
PALGRAVE

Palgrave in the UK is an imprint of Springer Nature Limited, registered in England, company number 785998, of 4 Crinan Street, London, N1 9XW.

Palgrave® is a registered trademark in the United States, the United Kingdom, Europe and other countries.

ISBN 978–1–352–00297–3 paperback

This book is printed on paper suitable for recycling and made from fully managed and sustained forest sources. Logging, pulping and manufacturing processes are expected to conform to the environmental regulations of the country of origin.

A catalogue record for this book is available from the British Library.

A catalog record for this book is available from the Library of Congress.

Contents

Acknowledgements

This third edition is a product of the reflexive learning process and development of ideas that writing and rewriting engender. It is also a result of discussing knowledge, perspectives and experiences with colleagues and students on a regular basis, and I would therefore like to thank them for contributing to my development as a teacher and as an author. I would also like to thank the fantastic team at Palgrave for their dedication and expertise in editing and producing this book, particularly the Editor, Helen Caunce, Editorial Assistant Rosemary Maher, and Production Editor Georgia Park. Finally, I would like to thank my husband Chris, my wider family and my friends for all their support.

Introduction

A fundamental part of academic study is reading the work of other people and using their ideas to develop your own. This book takes you through the process of using your reading (your source material) in your own essays, from deciding what to read to checking your work for mistakes. *How to Use your Reading in your Essays* explains things simply and clearly, gives you key points and practice activities, and uses real sources and student writing.

How to Use your Reading in your Essays shows you:

- how to decide on and search for suitable sources;
- how to understand and question what you read;
- how to stay focused and to know when you have read enough;
- how to know whether you have really understood what you have read;
- what notes to make to be able to use sources properly and effectively;
- why, when and how to use quotations;
- why, when and how to put what you read into your own words;
- how to compare and connect different sources in your writing;
- what words and phrases to use when discussing and referring to sources;
- which grammatical areas often cause problems in student writing;
- how to check your work for mistakes.

You can use this book in the way that suits you best, for example by reading it all through (with or without doing the practice activities) or by using the most relevant sections when you are reading for and writing an essay. Most of the advice and examples in this book also apply to reports and other types of written assignment.

An example of how to use your reading in your essays

Below are the first three paragraphs from an excellent undergraduate essay. Assignment types vary greatly, but the style of writing in this example essay will be common to many of them. We will look at different aspects of this essay throughout this book, and you can find the complete essay in Appendix 1, pp.173–178.

Look at the essay section and notice how the student has used what they have read (their sources). The essay section is colour-coded as described below:

Black	= student	student's own ideas, information and words
Light blue	= source	source ideas and information, using either the exact words of the text (quotations) or the student's own words (paraphrase or summary)
Dark blue	= in-text reference or reference reminder phrase	citation or phrase indicating that a source is being used.

Outline what business ethics is and discuss whether it is important. (2,500 words)

Over the past couple of decades, the issue of the ethical stance of businesses appears to have become more explicitly an area of public debate and consumer awareness. Two illustrations of this are the number of publications that give consumers information about a company's ethics (for example the Ethispere and Good Shopping Guide annual lists), and the fact that many large organisations now have an 'our ethics' tab somewhere on their website. The UK ethical sales market is currently valued at over £38 billion, and has been expanding year on year over the past decade, with current growth at about 8.5% (Ethical Consumer Research Association and Triodos Bank 2017). In this essay I will briefly define business ethics, and then consider whether it does and should have value as an aspect of both business activity and business theory and training.	Student's point

Sources used as evidence and support

Student's aims |
| Defining what constitutes a business is contentious in itself, but for the purposes of this short essay I will define a business as any profit-making enterprise, including charities (who make profits to invest back into the enterprise). Similarly, there are numerous, overlapping definitions of business ethics. Shaw and Barry (2007) define it as 'what constitutes right and wrong (or good and bad) human conduct in a business context' (p. 25). This is a broad definition that needs some refining in two areas. One distinction to make is that ethics is not the same thing as general morality. Crane and Matten (2016) explain that although morals are a basic premise of ethics, ethics and | Student's points

Sources used as evidence and support
Student's point |

ethical theory go a step further because they focus on how morals can be *applied* to produce explicit standards and rules for particular contexts, of which business is one. Ferrell, Fraedrich and Ferrell's definition of business ethics as the 'principles and standards that guide behaviour in the world of business' (Ferrell et al. 2002, p.6) is pertinent here, as it emphasises the application of morals to produce codes and guidelines.	Sources used as evidence and support
Codified ethical behaviour usually falls under what's called 'corporate social responsibility' (CSR), which in turn is usually seen as part of corporate governance,	Student's point
although there is overlap between the two areas of activity.	Student's point
The second aspect of defining business ethics which needs unpacking is that, as Crane and Matten point out, ethics is not synonymous with legality. They state that there is some overlap between law and ethics, but that legislation usually only regulates the lowest level of acceptable behaviour. In addition, as Trevino and Nelson (2010) state, the law is limited in what it can do to prevent unacceptable actions, because legislation follows rather than precedes trends in behaviour. Business ethics then, according to Crane and Matten, is mainly concerned with areas of conduct that are *not* specifically covered by law, and that are therefore open to different interpretations, a fact that means a particular behaviour may be legal albeit viewed by many as unethical.	Sources used as evidence and support
Combining all the perspectives outlined above, I define business ethics as . . .	Student's definition

et al. = and other authors.

Comments on how the student has used their reading in their essay

The student's own points

In these first essay paragraphs the student gives six of their own points and their general essay aims, and starts to give their own definition of business ethics. In each of the first two paragraphs the student first introduces their own point, then uses what they have read (their sources) as evidence and support, and finally makes their own comment and/or moves on to their next point.

You can see this 'source wrapping' sequence by looking at the general colour pattern of the first two paragraphs – black, blue, black. This pattern shows that the student is using sources as support for their own points and comments, rather than letting the sources take over their essay. The third paragraph also does this source wrapping in a way, but with the comment given as the first line of the fourth paragraph to act as a link between the two.

Use of sources

Note that in this essay extract the student uses only two short quotations; those of the definitions given in the second paragraph. In their complete essay the student quotes only five short sentences or sentence phrases and a few key terms; most of the time the student puts the sources into their own words.

Use of in-text references and reference reminder phrases

Every sentence in which the student uses a source contains either an in-text reference or a phrase to remind the reader that the source is still being used (for example, *They state that …*). The student does this not only when they give a quotation but also when they put a source into their own words. These in-text references and reference reminder phrases make clear to the reader which ideas and comments are the student's and which ones come from their sources.

The student has used an author and date system of referencing, and this system will be used throughout this book. The other main way to reference is to use a sequence of numbers and corresponding footnotes, called a numeric system. Examples of both referencing styles are given in Appendix 5, pp.203–205.

Part A
Understanding your reading

How do you decide what to read?

You will often have a reading list and guidance from your tutors on which sources are most relevant for your course assignments, but you will also be expected to find material independently. This chapter looks firstly at the terminology tutors use when they talk about sources, and secondly gives you advice on thinking about, finding and selecting material effectively.

What are 'primary' and 'secondary' sources?

Primary material is that which conveys an idea or information for the first time. Primary material can take any form: a laboratory experiment report, a survey, a letter, a YouTube video, a book or an academic article. Secondary material is that which uses, reports or discusses ideas or information already conceived of and communicated by its originator (the primary source).

There is a lot of confusion about the terms 'primary' and 'secondary' source, mainly because people think that these labels always refer to a whole text, which they do not. For example, a report that gathers and summarises information and then gives recommendations will be for the most part a secondary source, but will be the primary source of its own (new) recommendations. Another example is the academic journal article – this will be the primary source of the arguments, ideas and data given by the author, but will be a secondary source of anything the author uses that has already been published elsewhere. Even a student textbook, although mainly a secondary source of the knowledge it summarises and explains, will be a primary source of any original opinions or arguments put forward by its author.

Over to You 1
Is it primary or secondary data?

Below is an adapted extract of a research article in which the authors describe and discuss a study they conducted on dietary supplements (DS) taken by adolescents in Slovenia. Decide in which ways the extract is a primary, and in which ways a secondary source. (Note that the article uses a numeric style of referencing).

Article extract

The results of our study demonstrated that in the general Slovenian adolescent population, some of the reasons for using DS were clearly associated with the extent of PA [physical activity]. In contrast to these results, the only similarly conducted study performed until now in young adults[38] revealed no effects of exercise level on the reasons for using DS.

The current study demonstrated that in the general Slovenian adolescent population, males more strongly emphasized purportedly sports performance-enhancing effects of DS, whereas females were more concerned with preventing of illness and disease. This was true for both nonathletic and athletic adolescents. This was in accordance with other qualitative[4] and quantitative studies.[18,19,22] Of those studies, only 9 papers were found that reported percentages of adolescents/young adults, who stated specific reasons for using DS.

Adapted extract from: Kotnik, K., Jurak, G., Starc G. and Golja, P. (2017) 'Faster, Stronger, Healthier: Adolescent-Stated Reasons for Dietary Supplementation', *Journal of Nutrition Education and Behaviour* 49(10), p.821.

What is a 'reliable' source?

A reliable source is one where the information is as correct and complete as possible.

- **Named sources** can be assessed for credibility more effectively than anonymous ones because the trustworthiness of a source depends heavily on who has written it. This is important to remember with regard to website material; if you don't know the person or organisation who wrote the information on the website, you can't use it for academic work.

- **Checked sources** (also called peer-reviewed sources) will be more reliable than those that have not been checked. These are sources that have been assessed by experts in the field before being published (see 'academic and scholarly sources' below).

- **Non-biased sources** will be more reliable than more biased ones. For example, material published by political organisations might be biased, because the information will be manipulated and presented in a way that best suits the author's own purposes. Bear in mind, however, that no source can be entirely non-biased, and that even the authors of academic journal articles are trying to persuade you to a particular point of view, and so may manipulate ideas and facts slightly to suit their own viewpoint.

- **Current sources** are more reliable than older ones, simply because they *are* more up to date. You may want to read older sources that are key texts or to build up your knowledge, but for most topics you will also need current material. Always check online sources to see when they were last updated.

● **Primary sources** will be more reliable than secondary material. Authors of secondary sources might intentionally or unintentionally report the primary material incorrectly or in a biased way. In reality, it is not always possible or necessary to use only primary sources, but your tutor will expect you to read key primary material.

Top tip

Although the above holds true for the types of sources you will most commonly need for your assignments, you do need to think about what 'reliable' means for the type of information you are looking for. If, for example, your essay is about opinions in the media, then newspapers and television programmes will be reliable sources for this particular type of information, even though these sources may not be checked by experts and will be biased. Similarly, if you are writing about the views of different political organisations, then their leaflets and websites will provide reliable information on what these views are, even though such information may not be balanced or reliable in the general sense of the word.

What is an 'academic' or 'scholarly' source?

When tutors talk about academic or scholarly sources, they usually mean ones that have been peer reviewed, in other words, checked by an expert before publication. Most books undergo this peer review as part of the publishing process, and articles published by an 'academic', 'scholarly' or 'peer-reviewed' journal will have been sent to experts for review and checking. Tutors often use the terms *academic, authoritative, reliable, reputable, scholarly* or just *good* interchangeably to mean sources that have been checked in some way, or at least written by a subject professional (although *scholarly* can also just mean well written and researched).

Note that peer review is not the same thing as a film or book review. Book reviews are pieces in which the author gives their personal opinion, and include the book and article reviews commonly found towards the end of academic journals.

Is a reliable source the same thing as an academic one?

Although tutors sometimes use these terms to mean the same thing, you will see from the explanations above that an academic source is usually a reliable one, but that a reliable source is *not* always an academic one, as in the example of using a newspaper as a source of information on opinions in the media.

Non-academic sources

Below is a list of source types that are not academic and should not normally be used as source material for university essays:

➢ encyclopaedias (including Wikipedia);

➢ newspapers (including long articles in quality papers such as *The Times* or *The Guardian*);

➢ magazines (including quality magazines such as *The Economist*, *Newsweek* and *New Scientist*);

➢ news or TV channel websites (e.g. BBC News);

➢ trade publications and company websites;

➢ publications and websites of charities, campaign or pressure groups;

➢ student theses or essays;

➢ pamphlets and brochures;

➢ blogs and wikis.

How can you check that an online source is reliable and academic?

● Check your online databases, search engines and directories

Some online databases contain only peer-reviewed academic journals, but some of them also contain newspapers, magazines and trade publications, so read the database description to see what types of sources it contains. Be careful when using search engines such as Google or Yahoo, as they contain a mix of reliable, unreliable, academic and non-academic sources, and it can be hard to tell the difference. Google Scholar is better because it contains only literature related to academic work, but you still need to be careful, as not all of this literature is peer reviewed, and it also contains magazines and student theses.

● Check your websites

Be aware that just because an online article is well written, includes statistics and has in-text references, it does not necessarily mean that it has been peer reviewed. Similarly, words such as *journal, research or volume/issue number, Society or Research Centre* are increasingly being used by unreliable and non-academic websites. Always check the website's 'home', 'about us' or 'information for authors' pages to see if a journal peer reviews its articles before publication, and if you are still not sure, see what Wikipedia says about the journal.

   Take particular care when using online websites that are not part of a peer-reviewed journal. Do a bit of detective work by looking at the site's 'home' or 'about us' page, and/or by stripping back the URL to find the parent website, and also look at what Wikipedia and other websites say about the authors. The most important thing is to find out who wrote the information on the website, and remember that if you can't find who wrote it, you can't use it. Words that should warn you that an online article is probably not academic are: *magazine, digest, personals, news, press release, correspondent, journalist, special report, company, classified, personals,* and *advertisement.*

Wikipedia is useful for initial definitions and information, and for providing further references, but it is not reliable or academic enough to use as a source in its own right.

Over to You 2
Would you use these sources?

Read the descriptions below of ten potential sources for five different essay titles. Decide whether you think each source would be reliable or unreliable, reliable but not academic, or reliable *and* academic.

Sources for an essay on government support for people with disabilities

1   An article written in July 2010 in an online magazine called *Mobility Now*. It has news, information and stories and is a magazine for people with disabilities. It is published by a leading charity organisation for people with disabilities.

Sources for an essay on youth crime

2   A recent online article on ASBOs written by Jane Smith, Home Correspondent. The URL is the online business section of a national quality newspaper.

Sources for an essay on recent developments in stem cell research

3   An online article on stem cells, published jointly by three authors in 2011. The article has a date, volume and issue number. The article is on a website called 'Stem Cells'. This seems to be the title of the journal, and at the bottom of the page a publisher is given: Beta Res Press. In the 'information for authors' section, the website tells authors how to track the progress of their article as it goes through the peer-review process.

4   An online science publication that looks like a magazine. It has a news section, advertisements and job sections. It also has an issue and volume

number. It has an 'about us' page that describes how its correspondents obtain their information by contacting leading scientists, reading scientific journals and websites and attending conferences.

Sources for an essay on developments in animal cloning

5   An article from a printed booklet titled 'Animal Cloning' published in 2004. There is a series of booklets, each with a volume and issue number. Each booklet contains a collection of short articles and newspaper and magazine clippings which give a simple introduction to issues and public debate on a scientific topic.

Sources for an essay on business ethics

6   A well-written report (which starts with an executive summary) on business ethics in companies. The website is run by an organisation called SEB – Social Ethics in Business. On the 'about' page, the organisation describes itself as part of a network of business organisations that focus on corporate responsibility. Its funders and partners are large national and international business foundations and development agencies.

7   An online article entitled 'Business Ethics Guidelines'. The website address is 'Harold Jones International Company'.

8   An online article about McDonald's on a website called 'Centre for Management Research'. There is no 'about us' page but there is a homepage stating that the centre is involved in business research, management consulting and the development of case studies and training materials.

9   An online article on business ethics found on the website of the 'Centre for Business Ethics' of a university. On the centre's homepage it states that it helps businesses and the community, and offers workshops, conferences and lectures. It also states that the centre publishes its own *Journal of Ethics*.

10 An online article about a drinks company's activities in India. The article has no author but is well written and says 'for immediate release' at the top of the page. The website is given as a 'Resource Centre'. The 'home/about us' page states that the centre has evolved from networks and discussions by activists, and describes itself as a platform for movements to publicise their demands and apply pressure to governments.

(The articles and websites are fictitious but closely based on real examples.)

Five steps for deciding what to read

Step 1 Make sure you understand your assignment title

If you are reading for an assignment, break down the title and check that you really understand it. For example, does it ask you to develop an argument, give your opinion, use examples, or some of these things together? Does it ask for definitions, information on a process, advantages and disadvantages or for different views on an issue?

Rewrite the title in your own words – this is an excellent way of checking whether you really understand it. For example:

Essay title: 'Outline what business ethics is and discuss whether it is important.'

Student rewrite: *Give a brief overview of what business ethics is – define it. Then argue that business ethics either is or is not important, saying why you think this and backing up your argument with sources.*

Step 2 Think about what you already know

Think (and perhaps write down) what you already know and think about the essay question. For example, if you were preparing for the business ethics essay, you could first ask yourself what *you* think business ethics is and whether *you* think it is important.

You will probably already have done some reading on the essay topic during your course, so also think about how this information is relevant to your assignment title.

Step 3 Think about the types of sources you need

Don't be tempted to just type your essay title straight into an online search engine in the hope that something useful will come up. First think about what *type* of information and material you need – this will result in finding more appropriate sources more quickly.

Types of texts to consider might be:

➢ an introductory textbook to give you some initial ideas;
➢ chapters in more advanced textbooks;
➢ case studies to look at real-world examples;
➢ key established academic books and articles on the topic;
➢ more recent academic journal articles on new developments or ideas on the topic;
➢ original data from experiments or other research;
➢ non-expert and/or biased, subjective material.

In order to select appropriate source types you need to be aware of their purpose, whether they are reliable and whether they are primary or secondary sources. Below is information about this for four common text types.

Textbooks

For example: Crane, A. and Matten, D. (2016), *Business Ethics*

Textbooks are written for students to give them an understanding of basic concepts and ideas, and to give an informative overview of the subject. They are written in a formal but easy-to-read style. They are reliable sources of information, but be aware that textbooks:

➢ tend to give a simplified version of information and ideas;

➢ sometimes present an idea as fact when it is actually something that is debated and not agreed on by all experts in the field;

➢ sometimes do not give enough detail about the author/source of the information or ideas they discuss;

➢ are mainly secondary sources because they are giving an overview of primary sources. However, where the authors of the textbook give their own view of a topic the book is a primary source of that viewpoint.

Case studies

For example: 'Launching High-End Technology Products: A Samsung Case Study', http://businesscasestudies.co.uk

Case studies are either real-world or invented scenarios given as an example of a particular principle, situation or concept. Textbooks and student websites often give case studies relating to a particular topic, and other published case studies are written by organisations as an illustration of what they do.
   Be aware that case studies:

➢ sometimes describe real situations but sometimes use invented examples;

➢ should not normally be used as key sources for an essay because they are designed to be illustrative examples of a point rather than a source of information.

Reports

For example: *Ethical consumer markets report 2017*, Ethical Consumer Research Association and Triodos Bank, 2017

Reports compile or present an account of something. They are often written in order to give recommendations or to find a solution to a particular problem.
   Be aware that reports:

➢ are often requested (commissioned) by a person, group or organisation, and can be biased if the report has been asked for in order to persuade investors, shareholders, voters or other interested parties;

➢ can be a primary source of data the author has derived through their own statistical analysis (such as the financial performance of the business) or can be both a secondary source of the data it has collected from elsewhere and a primary source of the recommendations it makes.

Academic journal articles

For example: Carr, A. Z. (1968) 'Is business bluffing ethical?' *Harvard Business Review* 46(1), pp.143–153.

Academic articles are usually written by academics and/or practitioners in the field, and published in what are called academic or scholarly journals. Academic articles present an idea, argument, theory or model, usually supported by their own primary research, data and ideas produced by other academics in the field (secondary data), or a mixture of the two. Academic articles start with an abstract, which is a short summary at the start of the article laying out the context, issue and methodology. The abstract may or may not also give results and conclusions.

Be aware that academic articles:

➢ have abstracts, which are useful to help you decide whether you want to read the whole article, but that on their own should not be used as a source for your essay;

➢ are seen as reliable but might still be biased and misrepresent the information or ideas of other authors. If possible therefore, you should check the key primary sources cited;

➢ are sometimes written in an overly formal and academic style which can make them difficult to understand;

➢ have reference lists which you can use to find other sources on the topic.

As an example of thinking about source types before searching for material, the student who wrote the essay on business ethics on p.173 decided to look first for textbooks that would give definitions of business ethics. They also realised that they would need some relevant journal articles by key authors for views on the importance of business ethics, and also that they would need reports and government documents for specific data on business regulations and guidelines. Finally, the student decided it would be a good idea to look at some company websites in order to find out what businesses themselves say about their ethics.

Step 4 Do a first search

The process of finding source material is called a literature search, and is a vital part of academic research. As you search, keep checking that your sources are relevant and reliable.

Another point to bear in mind is that you will need different perspectives on the issue, and that you should try to keep a multi-perspective overview as you progress in your searching and reading, rather than become too focused on the first one or two sources you find.

Headings, content pages and article abstracts will help you decide whether a source is relevant. Reading just the introduction and conclusion is also a quick way of finding out whether a source will be useful, and the reference list at the end may provide you with details of further useful material.

Write down the details of each source you think you might use (author, date, title, journal/publisher) and where and how you found it, in case you need to find it again later (see p.40).

Step 5 Refine your search

When you have done your first search, think again about what you will want to say in your essay. This might change as you read more, but you will now probably have some idea of how you want to answer the essay title. Look in more detail at the sources you have found to see which of them are the most relevant, and to check whether you have any important gaps in your material. Check the usefulness of each source you have selected by asking yourself the following questions:

➢ What type of source is it, and who wrote it?

➢ Is it a reliable and academic source and if not, is that OK?

➢ Is it really relevant to specific points in my essay?

➢ Which chapters or sections of each source are most relevant, and are any sections not relevant?

➢ Why exactly am I going to read it?

➢ Do my sources give me different perspectives on the issue?

Top tips

● Spend time on really understanding your assignment title – a common cause of low marks is students not properly understanding what they are being asked to do, and occasionally this is because the assignment title is poorly written. Don't be afraid to ask your tutors about your assignment title, but don't simply ask them what it means; instead, tell them what *you* think the title means and ask them if your understanding is correct – this will show your tutor that you have done some thinking, and will lead to a more useful conversation.

● Do some detective work on any website you are planning to use to find out who wrote it – students quite often think a website is relevant and reliable when it isn't.

● Relevance, relevance, relevance. Keep asking yourself whether the source is relevant and why.

Summary

- Take some time to think about what types of sources you need and why.
- Rather than just typing in a word and seeing what comes up, make your online search as thoughtful and as focused as possible from the start.
- Be clear on whether each source is a primary or secondary source, or a mix of the two.
- Take advantage of the help your university library can give you.
- If you don't know who (or at least what organisation) wrote it, you shouldn't use it.
- Find sources that give different perspectives on the issue.

A2

How do you understand what you read?

By the time you have checked the reliability, relevance and purpose of a text, you will have a general idea of its content. The next step is to sit down and read in order to gain an accurate understanding of the material at both the surface level (words on the page) and the deeper, critical level. To do this you need to read in an active and questioning manner and to become really familiar with the text.

This chapter deals with understanding the words on the page, how to focus and how to know when you have read enough, and Chapter A3 looks at reading critically. Note that this division between surface and deep-level reading is somewhat artificial, and that in reality you will probably be reading at both levels simultaneously.

Seven steps for understanding what you read

Step 1 Order your sources

You can, of course, start reading wherever you like, but with limited time and the need to understand new information and concepts, you might find it useful to start with the sources you think are both central to your topic and easiest to understand. Understanding the words and ideas in easier material will help you to then understand more difficult texts.

Step 2 Approach the text actively: remind yourself why you are going to read it

Before you start reading something ask yourself *why* you are going to read it. For example:

- ➢ Are you reading to develop your general knowledge of the topic?
- ➢ Are you looking for an answer to a specific question or looking for specific facts?
- ➢ Do you need to follow and understand the author's argument?
- ➢ Are you looking for points to support what you are planning to argue?
- ➢ Are you looking for points which you will argue against?

Before you start to read a text, make some predictions about what the author might say. It doesn't matter if your predictions turn out to be wrong; the important thing is to become engaged and stay interested in what you read.

Step 3 Match your reading method to your reading purpose

In reality there simply isn't enough time to read everything from cover to cover, and you probably wouldn't want to anyway. In our everyday lives we read different things for different purposes and so read them in different ways (think about how you read a train timetable as opposed to a novel). You should apply the same principle to your academic reading, matching the *way* you read something to *why* you are reading it.

The three main ways of reading are:

➢ looking over a text quickly to find specific pieces of information (called scanning);
➢ reading something fairly quickly to get the general idea (called reading for gist, skimming or reading for breadth);
➢ reading something in detail (called close reading or reading for depth).

It is important to remember that scanning or reading for gist is *not* a substitute for close reading. You will need to do a lot of detailed reading for academic work, and one reason for only scanning or gist-reading some texts (or text sections) is to give you enough time for careful and close reading of others. You therefore need to develop the skill of recognising when it is appropriate to scan, when to read for gist and when to do close, careful reading.

Remember also to stay flexible about which reading method to use. You will often need to use a combination of methods, not just across different texts but also within a single text – zooming in and out. You might, for example, first quickly read over a whole text for gist, then read a section of it in detail, read some bits you find difficult again *very* carefully, and finally go back and scan the text for anything you think you may have missed.

As you read, you might also decide to change your reading approach. After reading about a quarter of the text, ask yourself, 'Is it giving me what I want? Do I understand what I'm reading?' If the answer to either of these questions is no, stop and think about why this is. It may be that you dived straight in with close reading and that it would be better to zoom out and get the gist of the text first before going back to the detail. It may be that you need to find an easier text as a way in to the topic, or it may be that the material is not as relevant as you thought and that you should stop and move on to something else.

Step 4 Use structure and language to help you understand the main message

Read the title, main headings and subheadings of the text. Read the abstract (if there is one), the introduction, the first sentence of each paragraph and the conclusion. Look up any key words you don't understand.

Use 'language signposts' (e.g. *Firstly, … .Secondly, …*) to help you identify which parts of the text are main points, which are more minor points and which parts are examples of the points being made; a mistake students sometimes make is to think that an example of a point is the point itself.

Step 5 Use structure and language to help understand what the author is doing

Re-read the text to clarify what the author is *doing*. For example, are they describing and giving information, explaining something, arguing against another viewpoint, stating their position or proposing and trying to persuade you of an idea? An author will probably be doing several or all of these things in different parts of one text.

Both the structure of the piece (heading, sub-headings, paragraphing) and its language will help you identify what the author is doing. In terms of language, pay particular attention to verb phrases, for example: *This article demonstrates … / This can be explained by … / Smith (2016) claims that … / This does not account for … / I challenge/dispute/ reject the idea that … / I would argue that ….*

Step 6 Understand accurately

After a first reading, read the text again and look up words and terms you don't understand rather than guessing what they mean. Here are some common text-reading pitfalls you should be aware of:

● **misunderstanding the meaning of noun groups**

Academic writing tends to use phrases that put several nouns together, and these can be difficult to interpret. In speech, the meaning of a noun group is conveyed by word stress, but in writing the author's meaning can be unclear. For example, three different possible meanings of a phrase are given below, with highlighting used to indicate the word grouping leading to each interpretation.

1 *A US megaproject funding committee* = A megaproject funding committee that is registered or operates from the United States.
2 *A US megaproject funding committee* = A funding committee that looks at US megaprojects.
3 *A US megaproject funding committee* = A committee that looks at US megaproject funding.

If you are unsure of the meaning of a noun group, read the surrounding text carefully to help you. For example:

> There have been several problems in recent years over how large, complex construction projects are financed in the US construction sector. This article will look at ways in which such irregularities can be monitored, particularly at the use of committees.

Reading the noun group in the context of its surrounding sentences tells us that the author's intended meaning is interpretation *3* above.

- **misinterpreting the main point of data**

  Students sometimes get bogged down in the detail of data given in tables, charts and graphs, and so fail to understand the key point. When presented with data, rather than start by analysing the statistics, take a few minutes to try to understand the point the author is illustrating and the overall message of the information. You can do this by reading and thinking about the diagram title, headings and sub-headings, and by taking note of what the author *says* when they introduce the data and when they comment on it afterwards. Once you have understood the overall point the author is making, you can zoom in and analyse the data in more detail.

- **misinterpreting or not noticing comparatives (e.g. *better*), superlatives (e.g. *best*) and degree (e.g. *slightly, very*)**

  For example, does the author say something is a good option or the best option? Do they say that a number is high or the highest? Does the text say something is as good as or better than something else? Does it say that something is marginally, relatively or highly significant?

- **not noticing the words *no* or *not***

  Pay careful attention to *no, not* and other phrases that indicate a negative – if you don't notice these words you might think the author is saying one thing when they are actually saying the opposite.

- **not noticing the difference between major and minor points**

  Pay attention to language that indicates major points, e.g. *the central issue here is . . . / the point I am trying to make is . . . / our key concern is . . .* and language that indicates more minor points, e.g. *an additional point is . . . / of less relevance but still worth noting is . . . / a more minor question is . . .*

- **mistaking examples for points**

  Another common cause of misunderstanding is to mistake an example of a point being made for the point itself. Look out for phrases indicating that an example is being given, e.g. *such as . . . / for example . . . / to give an illustration of this . . . / a case in point is . . .* and be aware that sometimes such phrases come after the example:

  > The relevance of the real-world moral imperative in business is arguably even more evident when we look at what happens when business entities do *not* behave ethically, and **the 2008 US financial crisis is a good example of this**.

  or are not used at all:

  > The relevance of the real-world moral imperative in business is arguably even more evident when we look at what happens when business entities do *not* behave ethically. **The US financial crisis of 2008** occurred because four main factors combined to create global financial chaos, and . . .

● **not noticing who says what**

Notice the differences between when the author is saying something and when they are discussing what someone *else* is saying. If you don't understand the difference, you won't understand the author's argument accurately.

Step 7 Become even more familiar with your material

Talk with colleagues and friends about what you have read, and question and reflect on how it compares to the views of other authors and to your own (see Chapter A3). Importantly, write about the material in different ways, particularly by writing a short summary (see Chapter A5). If you find that you can't summarise the main points of the text in simple language, it probably means that you don't yet understand it clearly.

Example text extract

Below is a text extract to demonstrate steps 4, 5 and 6 above. Words and phrases that help the reader understand the text are highlighted, and comments on this language are given in the right-hand column.

In this extract the authors look at the following question: 'Which aspects of child development best predict whether an adult is satisfied with life?'

Three key dimensions of child development are at work. One is intellectual development, which we measure by the highest qualification that the individual achieved. This is turned into a single variable using weights derived by regressing wages on highest qualification. A second dimension is behavioural, measured in the Rutter behaviour questionnaire by 17 questions answered by the mother. The third dimension is emotional health based on a malaise inventory (22 questions answered by the child and 8 by the mother).	The first sentence of the paragraph usually gives the topic
	These words introduce the three key dimensions
	Verb that tells you what the authors are doing
We now regress adult life-satisfaction on these three variables, as well as on family background. As Figure 5.4 shows, the strongest predictor of a satisfying adult life is not qualifications but a combination of the child's emotional health and behaviour. These findings have direct relevance to policy.	It is important to notice the words *not* and *but* here

But what, in turn, determines child development?... Our aim is to explain the three measures of child development. Intellectual development is now measured by GCSE scores. The emotional health of the child, however, has particular significance, since it is also the best measure we have of the child's own quality of life—it is a final product as well as an input into the resulting adult.

Sentence that gives the key question the authors are addressing

Verb indicating what the authors are trying to do

Note that this means it is the most or very significant

Figure 5.4 How Adults' Life Satisfaction is Affected by Different Aspects of their Development as Children: Britain. (Partial correlation coefficients)

Heading that gives the main point of the data

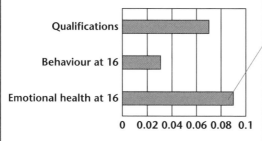

The point of the data is to compare the impact of the three factors at the age of 16 on life satisfaction as an adult. The key finding is that emotional health is the most influential factor

Source: Britain (BCS) Notes: Qualifications is the highest qualification that the person achieved. Behaviour at 16 is reported by the mother, and emotional health at 16 is reported by mother and child.

Clearly both parents and schools affect a child's development. **How, first, do parents affect their children's development?** ... As is well known, family income has a substantial effect on a child's academic performance, but a much smaller effect on the child's emotional health and behaviour. Father's unemployment has adverse effects, but is not that common. What is the effect if the mother goes out to work? If this happens in the first year, there are on average very small negative effects. If the mother works in subsequent years, however, it is positively beneficial for academic performance and further does no measured harm to the child's emotional health.

This question acts as a topic sentence

Note that this means an important and large effect

Not just smaller, but much smaller

It is important to notice the word *not* here

Not just small, but very small

It is important to notice the word *no* here

Adapted extract: Helliwell, J., Richard R., and Sachs J. (2017) *Happiness Report 2017*. New York: Sustainable Development Solutions Network, p.130.

How do you know that you have understood a text correctly?

This is a common worry. If you take the steps described in this section so far, you should be able to understand what you read, but no one can be sure they have fully understood what someone else has written. Both students and tutors check and deepen their understanding of a text by reading other material on the topic, by discussing it informally with colleagues and more formally in seminars, lectures and presentations, and finally by *using* their understanding to write summaries, essays and articles on which they can get feedback. As you go through this process yourself, you will correct yourself or be corrected by colleagues and tutors on any misunderstandings you might have, and will gain the confidence to recognise that you have understood things correctly. If you feel that you do need to check something particular, ask your tutor about it. Remember however, that different readers will interpret a text slightly differently, and so you might find yourself disagreeing with your tutor (not necessarily a bad thing).

How can you stay focused and not give up on a difficult text?

➢ Try not to be discouraged – most people find reading academic texts difficult, particularly when dealing with a new topic, and difficult texts will get easier as you build up your knowledge.

➢ Read actively and stay engaged – write down the questions you want to answer and keep these where you can see them while you are reading.

➢ On your first reading, look up key words, but save looking up other words for later so that you don't lose pace and focus.

➢ Pause briefly every few paragraphs to think about what you have just read.

➢ Make notes and/or use a highlighter to pick out key sections (see Chapter A5).

➢ Make a reading schedule: read at the times of day when you have high energy levels, create a calm (but not sleepy) reading environment, and read for intervals of 30–40 minutes with breaks of 5–10 minutes in between.

Top tip

Set up your own small face-to-face or online reading discussion group to talk about and check your understanding of texts. These groups can be invaluable in many ways, including helping you improve your participation in seminars.

How many sources do you need?

This is another common worry, and one to which there is no precise answer. The number of sources you need to read will depend on the course, your assignment, how much you know already, what you are reading, how you use your sources, and how much time you have. You should ask for guidance if you are unsure, but as a very rough guide, your tutor will expect you to read anything from around 8 to 15 different texts or text sections for a good 2,500-word essay. Much more important than the number of texts you read is their quality, currency, relevance and potential for giving you a fresh way of looking at your question. You need to have most or all of the different perspectives on the issue, and to have more than one source that can support each main point in your own argument; doing all of this is what is meant by reading 'widely' or 'extensively'.

You can stop reading when you feel you have enough material to answer the assignment title fully and well, and can compare, contrast and group sources to give a range of different perspectives. You will then be in a position to use your grouping of sources and the relationships you discover between them to develop and support your own viewpoint.

Summary

- Reading and thinking are where most of your learning and creativity will happen, so take reading seriously and make it a priority in your time-management schedule. A common reason students give for struggling with reading is that they don't or can't give enough time to it.

- Before plunging into a text, pause to think about why you are going to read it and what it is you want to learn from it, then match your reading method to your reading purpose.

- Keep engaged with a text by regularly reminding yourself why you are reading it. Reading actively will improve your understanding and further increase your interest in the subject.

- Start by reading short articles and sections of easier texts before tackling harder and longer ones. Not everything you read will be well written, and most people need to read complex texts several times. Material will become easier to understand as you build up your knowledge on the topic.

- You need to understand what you read fully and accurately – look up new words and develop and check your understanding by discussing and writing about your understanding in various ways.

- Keep a multi-perspective overview as you read rather than aligning too strongly or too early with one text and one perspective.

- Make useful notes on your reading (see Chapter A5).

- Reading about and understanding new ideas and information take effort; if your brain hurts a bit it probably means you are getting somewhere.

How do you question what you read?

What does 'reading critically' mean?

As well as understanding what you have read, you will be expected to analyse how the author uses key terms and to evaluate their evidence and argument. This whole process is what is meant by 'understanding at a deeper level', 'reading critically' or 'critical analysis'. Note that 'being critical' in this sense does not mean you have to say negative things about a text; indeed, you might want to be very positive about it. What it does mean is to question and to evaluate the text in a rigorous and objective manner.

What does 'analysing' mean?

To analyse means to break down, examine and question something (also referred to as *deconstructing*, *unpacking* and *examining*), with the aim of then using the results of this analysis to evaluate it. You should identify and then unpack the key terms, concepts and arguments of each author and text, and then also examine the relationships between different sources.

Analysis can be hard work because it is not something we do naturally; we tend to skip straight to evaluating (judging and forming an opinion). However, analysis is the foundation on which evaluation should be built; incomplete or poor analysis is a common reason for low marks in assignments.

What does 'evaluating' mean?

To evaluate source material means to use your analysis to compare the text's positive and negative aspects and its importance and implications, and so form a view as to its overall merit.

So, reading critically involves a process in which each stage builds on the previous one, as summarised in Figure 1 below.

Three steps for reading critically

Step 1 Identify and analyse the key terms and concepts

Take each key term and break it down to clarify how the author is using it. Look at how the author defines a concept and examine this definition. What is the core

Figure 1 The process of critically analysing a text

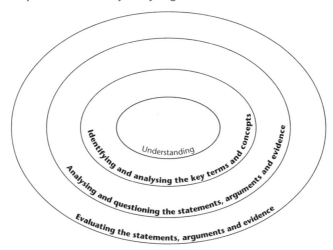

definition of the term? Are there any exceptional cases where the term would not apply, or borderline cases where the term only partially applies? Use such questions to refine your own definition and to compare it to that of the author.

An example of Step 1: student analysis of key terms used in a text about business ethics

Business: What types of business are we talking about? Are there any exceptions or borderline examples of 'a business' – for example, social enterprises, charities, trading where goods are exchanged but no profit is made? Does a business have to be profit-making? Is a business always the same as an 'organisation'? What are the differences between the two?

Ethics: Is ethics the same as morals or principles, law, beliefs? If not, how do ethics differ from these? Are there any exceptions or borderline cases of something being ethical? What is the difference between ethic and ethics?

Business ethics: Taking into account my analysis of *business* and *ethics*, how is the author using the term 'business ethics' – are they using it in the same way as other authors? How and why do different authors define business ethics, and what do these differences imply? Are there any exceptions or borderline examples which can help me refine my definition of business ethics?

Step 2 Analyse and question the author's argument

Ask yourself the following questions:

➢ What assumptions does the author make?

➢ Do I think these assumptions are correct?

➢ Are the stages of the argument clear and logical?

➤ Does the conclusion follow from the evidence given?

➤ How do the author's argument and position fit in with what I already know?

An example of Step 2: analysing and questioning

Below is the same extract as the one we looked at on pp.23–24. This time the annotations in the right-hand column are notes written by a student reader, showing their questioning of the author's use of terms, statements and argument, and showing what the student thinks they need to analyse in more detail.

We now regress adult life-satisfaction on these three variables, as well as on family background. As Figure 5.4 shows, the strongest predictor of a satisfying adult life is not qualifications but a combination of the child's emotional health and behaviour.[8] These findings have direct relevance to policy.	Key concepts for me to analyse: life-satisfaction/emotional health/emotional behaviour. Why do the authors combine these two factors in preference to qualifications? How are these findings relevant and to which areas of policy?
But what, in turn, determines child development? . . . Our aim is to explain the three measures of child development. Intellectual development is now measured by GCSE scores. The emotional health of the child, however, has particular significance, since it is also the best measure we have of the child's own quality of life—it is a final product as well as an input into the resulting adult.	What do they mean by *explain*? They don't explain the measures but rather examine their significance. I can see why emotional health is important, but why is it a final product and intellectual development is not? Surely they are both 'final products' that then feed into adult life?
Figure 5.4. How Adults' Life Satisfaction is Affected by Different Aspects of their Development as Children: Britain. (Partial correlation coefficients) 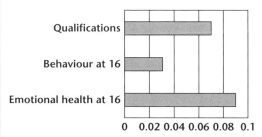 Source: Britain (BCS) Notes: Qualifications is the highest qualification that the person achieved. Behaviour at 16 is reported by the mother, and emotional health at 16 is reported by mother and child.	

Clearly both parents and schools affect a child's development. **How, first, do parents affect their children's development?** ... As is well known, family income has a substantial effect on a child's academic performance, but a much smaller effect on the child's emotional health and behaviour.	Why *clearly*? This is a big generalisation, although probably true. Still it is 'begging the question' – assuming something is true before trying to prove it. Is it well known? They don't give any references in support of this claim.

Adapted extract from: Helliwell, J., Richard, R. and Sachs, J. (2017) *Happiness Report 2017*. New York: Sustainable Development Solutions Network, p.130.

Step 3 Evaluate what the author says

Stand back and give the text an overall evaluation. In other words, weigh up the strengths and weaknesses of the author's argument and form a view on how important and/or useful the text is and why.

Ask yourself the following questions:

➢ What are the author's general way of thinking and position on the issue?

➢ What are they trying to do, and how well do they do it?

➢ Why do I think people would read this text, and do I think it is worth reading?

➢ What implications does the author's message have, and how might it affect knowledge and ideas in the wider field?

➢ Am I persuaded by what the author says? Why/why not?

➢ How do my background, experiences and viewpoint affect what I think about the text?

➢ How has the text developed, modified or perhaps completely changed my thinking?

➢ Will I use what the author says in my argument?

➢ Will it support my conclusion, or does it give an opposing viewpoint?

➢ Will I use it as an important piece of information or only as a minor source?

An example of Step 3: evaluating

Below are three short sections of a source the student used in their business ethics essay. The extract is followed by the student's informal written evaluation and reflection from their critical analysis of the whole article.

Extract

If one searches the literature, it appears that in the thirty years that business ethics has been a discipline in its own right a model of business ethics has not been proffered. This paper attempts to address this gap in the literature by proposing a model of business ethics that the authors hope will stimulate debate (see Figure 1). This model is one that is predicated on the tenets of developed countries operating within a capitalist paradigm.

. . .

Socially responsible managers do the right thing because it is the right thing to do. It is the correct action to take and an action that society expects. Executives should 'act ethically not out of fear of being caught when doing wrong. Rather, they should embrace ethical behaviour in business because of the freedom, self-confirmation, and success that it brings' (Thomas et al., 2004, p.64).

. . . it is important to see business ethics as a highly dynamic and continuous process without an end. A process, however, that is predicated on the interrelationship between business and society where each one is interdependent and responsible together for the outcomes. Hoffman and Moore (1982) suggest that the pre-eminence of business ethics is because of a perceived failing, by the general community, of business to act for the general good of the society. They, therefore, suggest that the mutual obligations of business to the community and the community to business need to be restated.

Extracts from: Svensson, G. and Wood, G. (2008) 'A model of business ethics', *Journal of Business Ethics* 77, pp.303–322.

Student's informal evaluation and reflection

The authors offer a model to show that managers should act ethically because they are intrinsically part of society. They look only at businesses operating in a developed world and a capitalist context, and presumably there are lots of businesses outside these types of context, but they don't mention these. Svensson and Wood also seem to assume that individuals and society always expect businesses to behave well and to trust them – I don't think they do. S and W also assume that there are socially responsible managers who want to do what is right – this might not be a correct assumption and they don't give any examples as evidence of this.

Svensson and Wood argue strongly and clearly that business and society depend on each other and so have a responsibility to each other to behave ethically. However, they seem to ignore the fact that not everyone thinks like this, and so their argument seems to be based on some unproven assumptions. Also, they leave out some other simple models of business ethics I've read about and they don't use real business examples for some of their points – they only make references to primary sources that have the examples. Also the article is now quite old, and I need to check whether they have written anything more recent or if other authors have developed or critiqued this model.

Still, it's a good persuasive argument – seems to be logical, well-structured, well-researched and expert. Their conclusion is supported by evidence, although this is mainly by reference to other authors – I will need to read a couple of these primary sources for myself. I think that I am partly persuaded by their points because it is also my view, so I am probably not being totally objective! Still, if anything, reading the article has developed my ideas by making me even more convinced that business ethics is crucial to us all in the wider social context. I think that this article is solid enough to use as one of my sources as evidence to support the idea of interdependence of business and society which I am starting to realise will be a key point in my argument.

Over to You 3
Question and evaluate this article

Below are sections from another article the student used for their business ethics essay. Read the sections and then question and evaluate them. You can't do this fully without reading the whole article, but you can still do some useful critical reading. You can compare your thoughts with those on p.180.

Is business bluffing ethical?

We can learn a good deal about the nature of business by comparing it with poker. Poker's own brand of ethics is different from the ethical ideals of civilized human relationships as the game calls for distrust of the other fellow . . .

That most businessmen are not indifferent to ethics in their private lives, everyone will agree. My point is that in their office lives they cease to be private citizens; they become game players who must be guided by a somewhat different set of ethical standards . . . The illusion that business can afford to be guided by ethics as conceived in private life is often fostered by speeches and articles containing such phrases as, 'It pays to be ethical', or, 'Sound ethics is good for business'.

Actually this is not an ethical position at all; it is a self-serving calculation in disguise. The speaker is really saying that in the long run a company can make more money if it does not antagonize competitors, suppliers, employees, and customers by squeezing them too hard. He is saying that overly sharp policies reduce ultimate gains. This is true, but it has nothing to do with ethics.

To be a winner, a man must play to win. This does not mean that he must be ruthless, cruel, harsh, or treacherous. On the contrary, the better his reputation for integrity, honesty, and decency, the better his chances of victory will be in the long run. But from time to time every businessman, like every poker player, is offered a choice between certain loss or bluffing within the legal rules of the game. If he is not resigned to losing, if he wants to rise in his company and industry, then in such a crisis he will bluff – and bluff hard. Whatever the form of the bluff, it is an integral part of the game, and the executive who does not master its techniques is not likely to accumulate much money or power.

Adapted extracts from: Carr, A. Z. (1968) 'Is business bluffing ethical?' *Harvard Business Review* 46(1), pp.143–153.

Critical and non-critical writing

Student writers sometimes put too much non-critical content in their essays, i.e. background information, description and explanation. In particular, they mistake explaining something for being critical. Explanation can seem like critical writing because it gives reasons and perhaps a conclusion, but it is still just a type of description and statement of fact; an explanation does not analyse, evaluate, argue or try to persuade.

Over to You 4
Is it critical or non-critical writing?

Look at the three adapted extracts from a student essay addressing the title '*Why do land-reform policies fail?*' Read each extract and decide whether the student is just describing or explaining what they have read, or is using their source critically.

Extract A

There are several reasons why land-use policies can fail, and one of the most important is a lack of involvement of the people living on the land. Aritia, Vlieta and Verburga (2018) look at the mismatch between the perceptions of farmers and local government and those of high-level government in how actively farmers are involved in policy. A second reason land reforms might not work is . . .

Extract B

There are several reasons why land-use policies can fail, and one of the most important is a lack of involvement of the people living on the land, as recent research suggests. For example, Aritia, Vlieta and Verburga (2018) look at the reasons for the lack of active participation in land policy by local farmers. Although the study looks at only one region in Ethiopia, it uses a large amount of data, providing solid evidence of the negative effects of a lack of local participation. Other studies that also show the importance of local involvement are . . .

Extract C

There are several reasons why land-use policies can fail, and one of the most important is a lack of involvement of the people living on the land. Aritia, Vlieta and Verburga (2018) look at the mismatch between the perceptions of farmers and local government and those of high-level government in how actively farmers are involved in land-use policy. The authors suggest that local and high-level government need to work together to ensure higher levels of farmer participation. A second reason for failure of land reforms is . . .

Extract D

There are several reasons why land-use policies can fail, and one of the most important is a lack of joined-up thinking between local and national governments and policies. In a recent study, Aritia, Vlieta and Verburga (2018) look at this problem in the context of the Rift Valley in Ethiopia, and demonstrate that a gap in perception between local and higher government departments can lead to ineffective land-use policies. One flaw in this 2018 study is that it uses only interviews as data. However, it still presents convincing evidence, and their conclusion is also supported by another major piece of research by . . .

Summary

Although you need to understand what the author says on the page, you also need to go beyond this level of understanding and decide what *you* think about the author's message. To do this you need to read critically: to analyse, question and evaluate what the author says.

Reading critically requires:

- understanding the text;
- understanding what the author is trying to persuade you of;
- identifying the key terms and concepts and examining how the author uses them;
- examining the logic of the argument;
- thinking about whether the evidence supports the conclusion;
- relating the ideas and information in the text to your own views and knowledge.

A4

How do you compare and connect what you read?

The whole point of taking a critical approach to reading is to use your analysis and evaluation of different authors' ideas to produce your own way of seeing the issue. This means that in addition to analysing each text separately, you will also need to analyse the relationships between texts, sometimes referred to as 'synthesising sources'. By examining the relationships between different texts and ideas you will make your own connections and see your own patterns, and so develop your own insights. 'To synthesise' means to combine two or more things in order to create something new, and putting your synthesis of sources together with your own ideas is also generally referred to as 'synthesis' and 'writing a synthesis essay'.

Note that you will only be able to synthesise your sources properly if you have first analysed and evaluated each source individually, and importantly, understood the position of each source author.

This chapter looks at analysing the relationships between source ideas (synthesising sources), and we will look at the final, broader synthesising process in Chapters B4 and B5.

Figure 2 The process of effective source synthesis

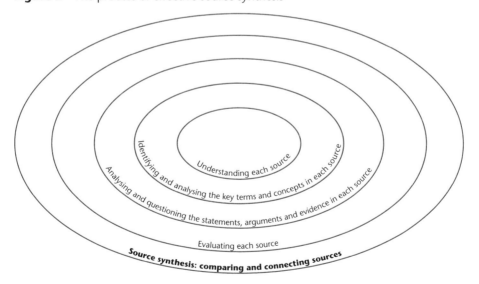

- Understanding each source
- Identifying and analysing the key terms and concepts in each source
- Analysing and questioning the statements, arguments and evidence in each source
- Evaluating each source
- Source synthesis: comparing and connecting sources

Five steps for synthesising sources

Step 1 Check how the different sources use terminology and primary material

➤ Analyse the way different sources use terminology, and be aware that different authors might use different terms for the same thing. For example, below are two definitions of business ethics that use different words to describe similar (although not identical) meanings:

'… moral and social responsibility in relation to business practices and decision-making'. (www.dictionary.com)

'… what constitutes right and wrong (or good and bad) human conduct in a business context'. Shaw and Barry (2007, p.25).

If you don't realise that different authors are doing this, you might think you are describing different viewpoints when you are not, and you might end up with an essay that is repetitive or nonsensical in parts.

➤ Check whether different secondary sources use the same primary source. It is quite common for different secondary sources to use and interpret the same primary source differently. Check for this, and if necessary read the primary material yourself to see what it says.

Step 2 Check that each source is relevant and productive

Check that you have related the different sources in terms only of the specific issue or question you are addressing. If you find a source is not directly relevant, discard it, no matter how long you have spent on it up to now.

Step 3 Check that you have a multi-perspective overview

Make sure that you have the different perspectives, arguments and counter-arguments involved in the issue; if not you might need to do further reading, as your essay will not be successful unless you show that you are aware of different viewpoints and address them.

Step 4 Compare and group your sources in relation to your question

Identify and analyse the relationships between your sources in relation to your specific point or question. Look at which authors agree with each other, which disagree, which partially or wholly overlap, which ones reinterpret or develop the ideas contained in other sources, and whether any authors have a unique position and/or are completely separate. Build up a picture of the location of different authors in the subject, and make notes, reflections and/or a source synthesis diagram to develop your thoughts on how the different texts fit together (see Figure 3).

Figure 3 Example of a source synthesis diagram

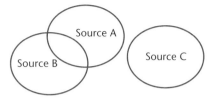

Step 5 Locate yourself in the issue

Think about where *you* currently sit in terms of the issue or question and why. Add your own location ● to your source synthesis diagram.

Figure 4 Example of a source synthesis diagram that includes your own location

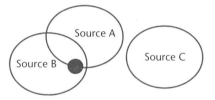

Over to You 5
Synthesise these sources

1. Read the short summaries of six of the sources used in the business ethics essay on p.173 and then compare and connect the sources. Decide which sources hold similar positions to each other and which do not.

Source summaries

Carr (1968). Successful businessmen need to play by the rules of the industry and these include 'bluffing' (lying) as an acceptable form of behaviour. This is part of legitimate business strategy, and business rules do not need to take account of personal or social principles.

Friedman (1970) in Fisher and Lovell (2003). The only important social responsibility business has to society is to increase profits and wealth. Corporations should not possess social responsibilities. This would be bad for business and society because it reduces profits and is unfair to shareholders.

Fritzsche (2005). Business ethics is good for businesses at all levels and underpins the market system because it creates the necessary exchange, trust, cooperation and productivity that organisations and the market need to function. Unethical behaviour destroys business.

Shaw and Barry (2007). Businesses are absolutely linked with the rest of society – they do not and cannot have morals that are separate from general morality.

Svensson and Wood (2008). The expectations of society influence business behaviour and therefore outcomes, which in turn are evaluated by society. Society and businesses are continuously and dynamically linked and have a mutual obligation to each other. Society needs to take more responsibility for what businesses do.

Wolf (2000). Corporate social responsibility is bad for the market because it takes business away from its primary purpose of making profits.

2. Create a source synthesis diagram

From your analysis of the relationships between the six sources, fill in the source synthesis diagram below by putting the initials of the source authors in the appropriate circles. A completed source synthesis diagram can be found on p.181.

Figure 5 Whether businesses should/have to behave ethically

Yes   No

Summary

- Synthesising sources means comparing, connecting and grouping them in relation to your own question and perspective, and is a fundamental part of all academic work.

- You can't properly compare and connect different sources unless you have first understood each one accurately and on a deep, critical level. You need to both think and write about your source material if you want to become really familiar with it and produce a successful synthesis. Use pictures, diagrams, rough notes, sticky notes, written reflections and any other form of notation or writing to help you develop your thoughts (see Chapter A5).

- Once you have discovered new relationships and patterns between the perspectives and ideas of different sources, you can use these discoveries to produce your own new insights.

Writing to understand your reading

The essay writing process is not a linear sequence of reading then thinking then writing. On the contrary, you should be thinking as you read, and doing such things as building up an annotated list of sources, making reflective notes during and after reading, scribbling down new ideas, and doing more reading after writing the first draft of your essay. Importantly, you will develop new thoughts and ways of expressing them even as you write your essay, and will probably still be developing your ideas after you have handed it in.

This chapter looks at some useful forms of writing you can do in preparation for your essay. They all relate to the aspects of reading and thinking we have looked at in Chapters A1–A4, but are presented together in this section so that you can see how early forms of preparatory writing can help you develop later ones. The forms of writing we will look at are:

● notes from reading;
● an annotated bibliography;
● a critical reflection of a source;
● source synthesis notes;
● a source synthesis reflection;
● a literature review.

Making notes

There's no point in making detailed notes of everything you read, and there probably wouldn't be enough time to do so anyway. A more realistic and effective approach is to use a combination of highlighting and annotating texts, making a few brief notes on main and interesting points, perhaps making more detailed notes on specific texts or sections of texts, and writing down your own thoughts and comments during or soon after reading.

So, although it's not effective to make detailed notes on everything you read, it can be useful to make meaningful notes on key texts or text sections. Making notes will help you:

● understand and become more familiar with your material;
● re-express, question and reflect on your reading;

- develop your own interpretation of the text;
- start using your own words;
- formulate your thoughts and connections with other pieces of knowledge;
- see how you might use your sources in your final essay.

Students who make some type of notes and written reflections usually get better marks than those who go straight from reading texts to writing their essay.

Five steps for making notes

Step 1 Have a clear purpose

To be effective, your notes need to follow the purpose you have for reading the text. For example, do you want your notes to:

➤ extract all the essential points and arguments?

➤ collect information on a specific theme?

➤ clarify the way the points relate to each other and see how the ideas are organised?

➤ reorganise or connect the text information in a new way?

➤ see where the author positions themselves?

Step 2 Write down the reference details

Build up a list of source details, including where, why, how you found them and other useful information and comments, sometimes referred to as a research record or research log. This log will form the basis of your bibliography, your critical reflections and your knowledge of the field in general and should be an essential part of your research process.

Example of a basic research log entry

> Djelic, Marie-Laure and Etchanchu, Helen.
>
> 'Contextualizing Corporate Political Responsibilities: Neoliberal CSR in Historical Perspective', Journal of Business Ethics, June 2017, Volume 142, Issue 4, pp 641–661
>
> Article is useful because it's current and gives a broad historical review of businesses and their role in society and politics.
>
> Found on 19/2/2018 by searching Google – Journal of business ethics – browse – volumes – 2017 at https://link.springer.com/journal/10551/142/4/page/1. Downloaded and saved on same day to my research files.

Step 3 Record when you are copying words and when you are using your own

This is important. Accidental plagiarism often starts when students use their notes in their essay, forgetting that the notes contain exactly or nearly the same words as the original text, or no longer being able to distinguish clearly between their words and those of the author.

So, create a recording method that allows you to distinguish between:

➢ exact words from the text (quotations);
➢ *most* of the same words from the text (close paraphrase);
➢ your *own* words to re-express ideas from the text (paraphrase);
➢ when the author is citing a different author;
➢ your own ideas or comments.

A common tendency when making notes is to copy down words and phrases with just a few changes, i.e. close paraphrase, so pay particular attention to recording when you do this in your notes; you will need to change the wording a lot more before you can use the information in your essay (see Chapters B2 and B3).

Step 4 Make your notes useful

People make notes in different ways (e.g. diagrams, flow charts, bullet points) and use different mediums (e.g. note-making software, paper, index cards). Whatever method you use, always:

➢ note down the page numbers and the date you make your notes in addition to the reference details;
➢ use abbreviations but write down what they stand for at the top of your notes;
➢ read carefully and make accurate notes – don't accidentally change the meaning of the text (see Chapter A2, pp.21–24);
➢ make clear in your notes which ideas are major points, which are more minor points of information, and which are examples of points;
➢ strike a balance between making notes that are not too detailed but also not so brief that they lose meaningful content and/or don't make sense when you read them later on.

An example of useful linear notes

Below are the student's notes from the sections of the Svensson and Wood article given on p.31.

Svensson, G. and Wood, G. (2008) 'A model of business ethics', Journal of Business Ethics, 77, pp.303–322. Notes written on 1/12/2012.	
p.305 true? no other models?	In 30 yrs. of BE (bus. ethics) as a subject, no model of BE. S + W want to fill this gap in BE theory, for debate.

p.310	'Socially responsible managers do the right thing because it is the right thing to do.'
does it? – not everyone does – generalisation.	Soc. expects the correct action. (CP)
p.319 (conclusion)	Mangs. should want to be ethical because it brings freedom and success. (S + W citing Thomas et al. 2004).
p.319 main point	BE – '... dynamic and continuous process ...' – 'interrelationship between businesses and society' – each responsible for the other.
key point re importance of BE	BE becoming impt. because people feel that buss. do <u>not</u> behave ethically – the 'mutual obligations need to be restated' (S+W, citing Hoffman and Moore 1982).

Comments on the notes

➢ The notes are brief but detailed enough to be meaningful. If the first line of the notes had been only *'In 30 yrs. no model – S + W want to fill this gap'* the student might later have been asking themselves questions such as '30 years of what?' 'A model of what?' 'What type of gap do they want to fill?'

➢ The student has a system for avoiding accidental plagiarism; they have used quotation marks when they have copied, the abbreviation 'CP' to indicate close paraphrase, nothing when they have used their own words, and a separate left-hand column for their own comments and thoughts.

➢ The student has noted when Svensson and Wood have cited other authors (Thomas et al. and then Hoffman and Moore). This will help the student avoid accidentally attributing the ideas of these other authors to Svensson and Wood when they use their notes in their essay.

➢ You can see that in making notes the student has naturally started the process of using their own words.

Step 5 Review and rework your notes

Look again at your assignment title and check the focus and relevance of your notes. Re-read and rework your notes as part of your analysis, questioning and evaluation of the text. Research has shown that students who review and reflect on their notes are more successful learners than those who don't.

Try one or more of the following:

➢ reworking your notes using a different format, e.g. rewriting linear notes as map/ diagram notes or vice versa;

➢ rewriting your notes to show how they relate to your assignment question title, adding comments and identifying any knowledge gaps;

> rewriting your notes to show how they relate to your own argument or perspective, adding comments and identifying any knowledge gaps.

Top tips for highlighting, annotating and making notes

- **Read first, note later** Try reading the text first without making any notes and then summarise the key points to yourself in your own mind and then on paper.

- **Don't use too much highlighter** If you do want to mark or highlight the text when you read, just pick out the most relevant sections by drawing a vertical line alongside them using a pencil, rather than a highlighter. This is a useful technique because you won't get a clear idea of the main points of the text until you reach the end, and if you highlight as you read for the first time you will probably mark up too much of the text. A better use of the highlighter is to use it later on to bring out and emphasise important information in your own notes.

- **Do more than just annotate the text** Annotating a text is fine, but try also to make some brief notes of your own so that you become more independent in the way you can re-express what the text says.

- **Make, don't take** Rather than copying down lots of individual sentences or chunks of text, try reading and thinking first and then creating your own notes by using some or all of your own words. You may be worried about 'moving away' from the text, of accidentally changing its meaning, or of the fact that you feel you can't put things into your own words as well as the original. However, you will need to re-express the text in your own words and style in your essay, and starting to do so at the note-making stage will help you gain practice and confidence in becoming more familiar with, and being more independent of your source.

Over to You 6
Make your own notes

Read and make notes on the extracts from the article by Carr given on pp.32–33, or use a short text of your own if you prefer. Read your notes a couple of weeks later and compare them with the original text. Check your notes for the following:

- Do your notes make sense to you – is their meaning clear?
- Can you distinguish between major and minor points?

- Can you distinguish between points and examples?
- Can you distinguish between places where you have copied, places where you mix your own and the author's words (close paraphrase), places where you have used your own words for the author's ideas (paraphrase) and places where you have noted your own comments and ideas?

If anything is unclear in your notes, think about how you could improve the way you make notes so that you would be able to use them accurately and effectively in an essay. You can compare your notes on the Carr article with those on p.181 although, as already stated, there is no one correct way of making notes.

Writing a critical reflection

This is a written reflection on your analysis, questioning and evaluation of a text, and any other thoughts and comments you have about it. You can write a reflection straight from your reading of the text and/or from any notes you have made. Writing a critical reflection will help you consolidate and restate the source information and ideas in your own words.

A reflection is informal and so can take any form you like, but it can be useful to use full sentences, as this will help you to start expressing yourself clearly in writing. Your reflection should include a short summary of what you have learnt, and if the text has diagrams, charts or tables, try also to summarise the key points of this data. For an example of a critical evaluation and reflection, look again at the one at the bottom of p.31.

Writing an annotated bibliography

An annotated bibliography is your own written list of the sources you have read (with full reference details) plus your own short summary and evaluation of each one. Compiling an annotated bibliography as you read different sources will help you to:

- develop your familiarity with your material using your own words;
- develop your critical evaluation of your sources;
- provide you with an overview of your sources so that you can compare and connect them and start to see how and why you might use them (i.e. synthesise);
- keep track of what you've read and remind you what each source is about;
- see if there are repetitions or gaps in your knowledge.

Example of an annotated bibliography entry

> Helliwell, J., Laylard, R., & Sachs, J. (2017) *World Happiness Report 2017*, New York: Sustainable Development Solutions Network.
>
> Edited book containing an overview by the editors, and then six chapters on different themes or areas of happiness in society. The report's main aim is to try to measure happiness in different countries and it supports the 2011 UN resolution of measuring happiness to inform social policy, although the editors state that they write as individuals, not representatives of the UN. The six factors identified by the editors as most influencing social happiness are: GDP per capita; health; life expectancy; support from friends and family; level of trust in government and business; feeling free and how giving/generous the society is. Chapter 2 looks at social happiness and ranks 155 countries. The other chapters look at China, Africa, America, key determinants of happiness and happiness at work. The report is very well researched and written, although I think that chapters on SE Asia, South America and Europe would have been useful.

Writing source synthesis notes

By the time you have read several sources and perhaps made some notes, a critical reflection, and an annotated bibliography entry for each one, you will already have starting thinking about how the different sources relate to each other. At this stage you might find it useful to make some synthesis notes and/or a source synthesis diagram.

As an example of source synthesis notes and diagram, below is one showing the relationships between the six sources summarised on pp.37–38.

Figure 6   Whether businesses should/have to behave ethically

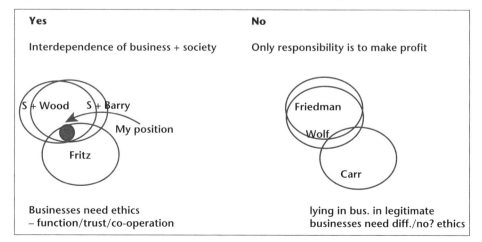

Writing a source synthesis reflection

You can use your synthesis notes to write a fuller reflection. A synthesis reflection is like a critical reflection but reflects on the relationships between sources rather than on an individual text.

Example of an informal source synthesis reflection

> Svensson and Wood take a similar position to that of Esty, Collins, Shaw and Barry and on the opposite side to Freidman, Wolf and Carr. The article says exactly the same thing as Shaw and Barry – that business cannot have morals that are separate from general morals but interestingly, S&W don't reference S&B, who published one year earlier – probably because S&W work in a different country and were offering a more theoretical perspective than S&B and also perhaps had not read S&B before they sent off their article to be published.
>
> S&W go further than S&B because they offer a detailed model as to how interdependence between society and business happens, and they also emphasise the dynamic aspect of the relationship between society and business. Importantly, it's also the only source I have read that states that because of this mutual influence and obligation society should take more responsibility for business behaviour.
>
> Generally, this article fits in with what I think about the importance of business ethics. The authors put forward a theoretical model which they say has not been done before and that it is therefore doing something new, i.e. filling a gap in theory. They expect other academics to argue or disagree with their model of business ethics.

Writing a literature review

A literature review (or survey) is a piece of writing that synthesises the key research on a specific issue or question. The review should summarise the various sources in a balanced way, and group them so as to provide the reader with an overview of how the ideas in the field have developed and of current areas of debate.

The length, amount of detail and level of critical evaluation in a literature review will vary according to its type and purpose. A literature review can range from a chapter in a dissertation tracing the development of ideas in the field and evaluating this research, to a shorter 'stand-alone' assignment, or a very short review that forms part of the introduction of an essay.

What many tutors mean when they ask students to write a literature review as part of an essay introduction is not in fact a full survey of the literature, but a short, synthesised (grouped) summary of relevant key sources that provides an overview of the main ideas in the field, and sets the scene for the student's own argument. This type of literature review should therefore finish by stating where the current essay fits into the field, and perhaps how it intends to address or fill an identified gap in the research.

Example of a short literature review

As an example of a very short literature review, below is the first section of a student essay about Travel Demand Management (TDM) measures.

> The rapid rise in car use since the 1950s has created a global transport challenge. Even though cars are both a comfortable and convenient mode of transport, they contribute to global warming, air pollution, depletion of fossil fuels and land-use fragmentation (Loukopoulos et al., 2005; Gärling and Schuitema, 2007; Eriksson et al., 2010). In a closely linked area of recent research, Gärling and Schuitema, 2007 and Graham-Rowe et al., 2011 confirm that cars are also principally responsible for the CO2 transport emissions, and that they also contribute to reducing quality of life by increasing noise, congestion and risk of traffic accidents. A set of measures aimed at reducing car use and therefore the above environmental effects are Travel Demand Management (TDM) measures. These have been developed and enhanced over the last decade or two, and a definition of success for these measures is significant progress towards reducing car use or changing use in a 'positive' way (Gärling et al., 2002; Loukopoulos et al., 2004; Loukopoulos et al., 2005; Gärling and Schuitema, 2007). This essay aims to examine how effective TDM measures have been in the specific context of major Chinese cities.

Two mistakes to avoid when writing a literature review

Listing sources

Students sometimes just list rather than group their sources, and/or jump from the review to their essay thesis without giving a linked literature context. As an example, below is a version of the above essay extract to show how much poorer it would have been if the student had just listed their sources and had not included the literature that relates directly to the aims of their essay.

> … Even though cars are both a comfortable and convenient mode of transport, they contribute to global warming (Loukopoulos et al., 2005). Cars cause air pollution (Gärling and Schuitema, 2007). Eriksson et al., 2010 show that vehicles contribute to depletion of fossil fuels and land-use fragmentation. A large amount of CO2 transport emissions are produced by cars and they reduce quality of life by increasing noise, congestion and risk of traffic accidents (Gärling and Schuitema, 2007). Graham-Rowe et al., 2011 have done studies on car CO2 emissions. This essay aims to examine how effective Travel Demand Management measures have been in the specific context of major Chinese cities.

Adding your own comments within the review

By grouping and linking your sources you are already commenting on them in a way, but you should not give explicit comments or points within your review, as the reader will not expect them and is likely to mistake them for source paraphrase. As an example of this, below is another modified version of part of the essay extract, into which I have added a comment (highlighted in bold). If such a comment had been part of the student's short literature review, the tutor might have thought that it was a comment given by Garling and Schuitema or Graham-Rowe et al. rather than the student's own.

> … In a closely linked area of recent research, Gärling and Schuitema, 2007 and Graham-Rowe et al., 2011 confirm that cars are also principally responsible for the CO_2 transport emissions, and contribute to reducing quality of life by increasing noise, congestion and risk of traffic accidents, **although the data for one of the studies need further analysis**. A set of measures aimed at reducing car use and therefore the above environmental effects are Travel Demand Management (TDM) measures. …

Summary

- Writing of any kind and at any stage of assignment preparation will help you to clarify your understanding of your reading and develop your own ideas.
- Read and understand first, make notes later.
- Don't spend too long writing detailed notes, as this can be an overwhelming and unnecessary task – make brief summary notes and more detailed ones only when necessary.
- Don't take notes, make notes.
- Use your reading, highlighting, annotations and notes to write short summaries, annotated bibliography entries, critical reflections, synthesis diagrams and literature reviews.
- Whatever type of notes or writing you are doing, have a method for recording the differences between copied phrases and your own words and ideas.

Part B

Using your reading in your essay

Why and how should you quote?

A quotation is an unchanged phrase, sentence or larger piece of text. As an example, below is a short extract from a student essay, with the quotation highlighted in blue.

> The study of ethics involves looking not just at whether behaviour in one part of society affects another, but at how people behave towards each other. As Trevino and Nelson (2010) state, 'Ethics is not just about the connection we have to other beings – we are all connected; rather, it's about the quality of that connection' (p.32).

Why use quotations?

Quotations are useful for helping you to:

➤ give a definition;
➤ state a fact or idea which the author has expressed in a unique and powerful way;
➤ establish or summarise an author's argument or position;
➤ provide a powerful and interesting start or end to your essay.

When should you not use quotations?

Use quotations sparingly and for the right reasons. Don't quote someone just because:

➤ you think that putting quotations in will make your essay look impressive and academic;
➤ articles you have read use quotations so you think you should also put some in your essay;
➤ you have written half of your essay and haven't used any quotations and so think you should put some in;
➤ you haven't given enough time to reading critically and making notes and so it seems easier to cut and paste some quotations into your essay rather than put the ideas into your own words.

How many quotations should you use?

Students sometimes think that good academic writing should contain a lot of quotations, but this is not the case. Most of the time you should restate sources using your own words (see Chapters B2 and B3). In the business ethics essay on pp.173–178 for example, quotations constitute only 4 per cent of the total assignment. An essay might not have any quotations but still be a successful piece of work because the author has re-expressed their source material effectively in their own words, and indeed, using too many quotations (for example for more than a quarter of your essay) might be seen as poor scholarship or even as a form of plagiarism, because a significant proportion of the essay consists of other people's exact words and style.

The appropriate number of quotations to use will vary according to the subject and type of assignment. For example, in literature and language assignments, quotations are often used more extensively because the language under discussion needs to be presented to the reader. Similarly, law assignments tend to use long quotations in order to cite extracts from legal documents. If you are worried about how many quotations to use, look at how they are used in your discipline, and also read the style guidance in your course handbook and ask your tutor about appropriate use of quotations. Whatever your discipline, topic or type of assignment, you should always ask yourself *why* you are quoting rather than how much.

Four steps for using quotations effectively and correctly

Step 1 Make effective notes

Being able to use quotations well usually stems from selecting and reading critically, making meaningful notes, and reflecting on your reading.

Step 2 Ask yourself why

Before you put a quotation into your essay, ask yourself why you are putting it in. Is it special enough? Is it really relevant to your point? Would it not be better to put it into your own words?

Step 3 Check for accuracy and give it a reference

When you have written your first draft, read each quotation and its surrounding sentences slowly and carefully. Make sure you have not taken the quotation out of context and/or misrepresented the author. Once you are sure that your quotation is worth putting in, check that you have quoted accurately, that you have used quotation marks *and* an in-text reference, and that you have used the correct grammar and punctuation before, during and after the quotation (see pp.56–57).

Step 4 Make a comment

Introduce your quotation in some way and comment on it, showing your reader why you have used it and how it is relevant to your own point.

Looking at examples of effective quotations

Below are three slightly adapted extracts from the business ethics essay on pp.173–178. Think about why the student decided to use the quotation in each case and then read the comments that follow the extracts.

1 Shaw and Barry (2007) define business ethics as 'the study of what constitutes right and wrong (or good and bad) human conduct in a business context' (p.5). Another definition describes business ethics as the 'principles and standards that guide behaviour in the world of business' (Ferrell et al., 2002, p.6).

2 Carr (1968) suggests that business rules do not need to take account of personal or social principles. Prindl and Prodham (1994), although not sharing this view themselves, point out that 'Finance as practised in the professions and in industry is seen as a value-neutral positive discipline, promoting efficiency without regard to the social consequences which follow from its products' (p.3).

3 My first point, then, is that businesses actually need to behave in an ethical manner in order to function properly. This idea is supported by Fritzsche (2005) and expressed succinctly by Collins (1994) when he states that 'good ethics is synonymous with good management' (p.2).

Comments

The student decided to quote in extract 1 in order to give examples of different academic definitions of business ethics. In extract 2 the student quoted Prindl and Prodham because they felt that it was a succinct and powerful way of expressing the fact that many people in the business world do not feel the need to take an ethical approach. In extract 3 the student used the quotation to support the first main point of their essay, and also because Collins's statement was a very clear and powerful summary of the idea.

Note that in all three extracts, the student introduces the quotation in some way so that the reader understands why it is being used. In other parts of their essay the student quotes two individual words, *bluffing* and *dysfunctional,* because they feel that these are key words used for a particular purpose by the respective authors (see p.58).

Common content errors

The four most common and serious mistakes students make with the content of quotations are:

➢ using a quotation that is not special enough and where they should therefore have used their own words. This includes common facts or knowledge, which don't usually need to be quoted;

➢ using a quotation that does not directly support their own point;

➢ not introducing or showing clearly why they have used the quotation;

➢ using a reporting verb (e.g. *state, show, suggest*) that is not correct for the context and function of the quotation (see Part C, pp.97–99).

Over to You 7
Would you use these quotations?

Below are some quotations from different student essays on bioscience topics. Read them and identify which of the above mistakes the students have made. Answers can be found on p.182.

1   Kzanty (2004) states that 'Organs such as the heart, liver, small bowel, pancreas and lungs are used for transplants' (p.11).

2   Logan (1999) states that 'The second world war ended in 1945' (p.111).

3   The main benefit of organ transplant is that it saves lives. As stated by Smith (2005), 'heart transplantation can save lives, but the procedure carries serious risks and complications and a high mortality rate' (p.12).

4   Improvements in transplantation have made it possible for animal organs to be used. This is beneficial, as patients are not forced to wait for transplants. As stated by Kline (2005): 'advances in genetic techniques mean that there is less chance of animal organs being rejected by the human immune system' (p.53).

5   Transplantation carries the risk of being attacked by the immune system and the patient is therefore at risk of organ failure again. As stated by Smith (2005): 'Everyone reported common side effects which included diarrhoea, oedemas, fatigue and ulcers' (p.5).

Common referencing errors

Three potentially serious mistakes students make when referencing quotations are:

● **not using *both* quotation marks and an in-text reference**

Some students make the mistake of using quotation marks but not giving the quotation an in-text reference, because they think that using quotation marks and also having a reference list at the end of their essay is enough. However, you must always give quotations both quotation marks (or indentation for long quotations) *and* an in-text reference. This is because the rules of academic writing dictate that something with an in-text reference but without quotation marks is a paraphrase, i.e. the essay-writer's own words and style. Therefore, referencing but not also using quotation marks is plagiarism, because you are in effect claiming someone else's words and style as your own. Look again at the essay extracts on p.53 and notice how the student uses both quotation marks *and* an in-text reference with each quotation.

- **giving a primary source reference for something found in a secondary text**

You must make clear to your reader which source you have actually read. For example:

> Hoffman and Moore (1982) suggest that the public feels that businesses fail to behave in a socially acceptable manner and that 'the mutual obligations of business to the community and the community to business need to be restated' (Hoffman and Moore 1982, cited in Svensson and Wood 2008).

Here the student correctly uses the phrase *cited in* to show that they did not read the Hoffman and Moore article but read the quotation in the article by Svensson and Wood. It would be poor scholarship and a misrepresentation of what they have read to give only the reference for Hoffman and Moore. This rule applies to quotation, paraphrase and source summary.

- **putting parentheses (round brackets) in the wrong place**

In the extract below notice that for the first quotation the student uses parentheses only for the year of publication and page number, because they are using the authors as the subject of their introductory sentence. For the second quotation, however, the student does not use the authors as part of their sentence and so puts both the names and year of publication in parentheses at the end.

> Shaw and Barry (2007) define business ethics as 'the study of what constitutes right and wrong (or good and bad) human conduct in a business context' (p.25). Another definition describes business ethics as the 'principles and standards that guide behaviour in the world of business' (Ferrell et al. 2002, p.6).

Over to You 8
Are these quotations referenced properly?

Below are four incorrect versions of the first quotation in the essay extract on p.53. Look at these altered versions and identify what the mistakes are in how the quotations have been referenced. Answers can be found on p.182.

1   Business ethics is the study of what constitutes right and wrong (or good and bad) human conduct in a business context.

2   Shaw and Barry (2007) define business ethics as the study of what constitutes right and wrong (or good and bad) human conduct in a business context (p.25).

3 Business ethics is 'the study of what constitutes right and wrong (or good and bad) human conduct in a business context'.

4 (Shaw and Barry 2007) define business ethics as 'the study of what constitutes right and wrong (or good and bad) human conduct in a business context'.

Common structure, grammar and punctuation errors

Don't worry too much about making small mistakes with the grammar and punctuation of quotations, but do try to develop correct use over time. The most common mistakes students make in these areas are:

● **Changing words or other elements in the quotation**

You must not change any words or spellings in a quotation. If the original text contains a mistake or non-standard usage in the quotation, you can add *sic* in square brackets immediately after the item to inform your reader that it is not your mistake. *Sic* is the abbreviated form of the Latin phrase *sic erat scriptum*, meaning 'thus was it written'. For example:

> The guidelines (EOI 2018) state that 'staff should discuss all problems with there [sic] manager'.

● If you need to add a word of your own to make the quotation fit in with your surrounding sentence or to clarify its meaning, use a square bracket to show that you have added something that was not in the original text. For example:

> Emille (2002) states that 'they [the public] only hear what they want to hear' (p.10).

The one change you are allowed to make without using square brackets is to change the first letter of a quotation from upper to lower case, so that your quotation integrates smoothly into the rest of your sentence. If you want to leave out part of a quotation, use an ellipsis (three dots with a space in between each one) to indicate that you have done so.

As an example of these last two points, below is an extract from the article by Albert Carr followed by a quotation used in a student essay. In the quotation, the student has used an ellipsis and has also changed the first letter of the quotation from 'T' to 't' so that it fits into their own sentence.

Source extract:

> The illusion that business can afford to be guided by ethics as conceived in private life is often fostered by speeches and articles containing such phrases as,

'It pays to be ethical,' or, 'Sound ethics is good for business.' Actually this is not an ethical position at all; it is a self-serving calculation in disguise.

Carr, A. Z. (1968) 'Is business bluffing ethical?'
Harvard Business Review 46(1), p.143.

Quotation from the extract used in the student essay:

Carr (1968) states that 'the illusion that business can afford to be guided by ethics … is a self-serving calculation in disguise'.

You do not usually need to use an ellipsis to show that you have missed out the start of the sentence in a quotation, as long as this does not lead to a misrepresentation of what the author says; if it does then do use an ellipsis to start the quotation. The use of ellipses varies slightly between different referencing styles, so check your referencing guide.

● putting in an extra *he/she/it/they* or topic word before the quotation

If you use the author's name as the subject of your introductory sentence you do not also use a subject pronoun such as *he* or *it*. Equally, if you use the topic word (e.g. 'business ethics') in your introductory sentence, you should not repeat it in the quotation.

● using the wrong punctuation in front of a quotation

Use a colon if you use a phrase that could stand alone as a sentence to introduce the quotation. For example:

Carr's central maxim is very clear: 'To be a winner a man must play to win' (p.153).

Use a comma if you use an incomplete phrase to introduce the quotation. For example:

As Tomalin (2010) states, 'Pepys was … mapping a recognizably modern world' (p.148).

According to Brandon (2008), 'History is a record of relationships' (p.151).

Don't use any punctuation if you integrate your quotation smoothly into the rest of your sentence. For example:

This idea is expressed succinctly by Collins (1994) when he states that 'good ethics is synonymous with good management' (p.2).

● putting punctuation marks in the wrong place at the end of a quotation

Keep question marks and other punctuation from the original text inside the quotation marks. The exception to this is the full stop; for the author and date in-text reference style you should put the full stop at the very end, after the page-number brackets.

Using quotation marks for single words

1 You might need to quote a word an author uses because they have invented the term or used a word in a special or novel way. It is common now to use either single quotation marks or italics for such terms. For example:

> Two key terms Freud developed were 'psychosis' and 'repression'.

> Two key terms Freud developed were *psychosis* and *repression*.

2 If you are not quoting from any particular source but want to talk about a word explicitly, you can also use single quotation marks or italics. For example:

> 'Visualisation' and 'smart content' are two buzz words currently used in digital marketing.

> *Visualisation* and *smart content* are two buzz words currently used in digital marketing.

If you want to convey the fact that you disagree or disapprove of how a word has been used, you can give it single quotation marks. These are often referred to as 'scare quotes', and work in the same way as putting *supposed* or *so-called* before a word. For example:

> No data are given in the report to support the so-called significant progress mentioned many times in the document.

> No data are given in the report to support the 'significant progress' mentioned many times in the document.

Note that you should be cautious of using scare quotes, as they convey a somewhat sarcastic attitude, which is not normally appropriate in academic writing.

Over to You 9
Are the grammar and punctuation of these quotations correct?

Below is one an extract from the business ethics essay followed by four incorrect versions. Identify the mistakes in each version. Answers can be found on p.182.

Correct essay extract*

My first proposition is that businesses actually *need* to behave in an ethical manner. This idea is expressed succinctly by Collins (1994) when he states that 'good ethics is synonymous with good management' (p.2).

Incorrect versions

1   My first proposition is that businesses actually *need* to behave in an ethical manner. This idea is expressed succinctly by Collins (1994) when he states that 'good business ethics is synonymous with good management' (p.2).

2   My first proposition is that businesses actually *need* to behave in an ethical manner. This idea is expressed succinctly by Collins (1994) when he states that 'good ethics is good management' (p.2).

3   My first proposition is that businesses actually *need* to behave in an ethical manner. This idea is expressed succinctly by Collins (1994) when talking about good ethics that 'good ethics is synonymous with good management' (p.2).

4   My first proposition is that businesses actually *need* to behave in an ethical manner. This idea is expressed succinctly by Collins (1994) when he states that 'good ethics is synonymous with good management.' (p.2)

*The answers on p.183 also include a correct version of this extract using the numeric referencing system.

Summary

● Save quotations for special occasions – you do not have to put them in just to make your work look academic.

● It is usually more effective to put source information into your own words (paraphrase) than to quote.

● Always check that a quotation is specifically related to the point you are making.

● Always comment on a quotation explicitly so that your reader is clear about why you are using it.

Why and how should you paraphrase?

Paraphrasing is when you restate source material using your own words and style. The term paraphrasing is commonly used to refer to the rewriting of a specific idea or piece of information contained in a short section of text, although summarising a source is also a form of paraphrase. In your writing you will often need to paraphrase, but it is a complex skill that takes time and practice to acquire. Importantly, in order to paraphrase effectively you need to have a good understanding of your source material.

Why paraphrase?

Conveying an idea or point from a source using your own words and style allows you to:

➤ understand and think about what you have read in a more independent way;

➤ express the information and ideas from sources in your own style of thinking and writing so that you can integrate them smoothly into your argument and essay;

➤ restate information and ideas from sources in a way that best supports your own argument;

➤ show your tutor that you have understood what you have read and how you have used it to develop your knowledge and ideas;

➤ express information and ideas from complicated texts more clearly and simply;

➤ restate information and ideas from your sources that are not special enough to quote.

Looking at examples of effective paraphrases

Below are two book extracts, each followed by an essay extract in which the student introduces their own point and then paraphrases from the source text (the paraphrases are in shaded light blue). Compare the essay extracts with the source material and then read the comments on them.

Source extract 1

… amazon.com currently stocks more than 14,000 books related to business ethics and corporate responsibility, whilst a Google search on 'business ethics' returns more than

4 million hits at the time of writing. … One annual UK survey, for instance, estimates the country's 'ethical market' (i.e. consumer spending on ethical products and services) to be worth something like £35bn annually (The Co-operative Bank 2008).

> Extract from: Crane, A. and Matten D. (2010) *Business Ethics*, p.14.

Essay extract 1

Over the past couple of decades, the ethical credentials of businesses appear to have become an explicit factor in consumer choice. The UK ethical market is valued at over 30 billion euros per year, and there are currently over 14,000 books and 4 million web entries related to business ethics (Co-operative Bank 2008, cited in Crane and Matten, 2010).

Source extract 2

… there is indeed considerable overlap between ethics and the law. In fact, the law is essentially an institutionalisation or codification of ethics into specific social rules, regulations, and proscriptions. Nevertheless, the two are not equivalent. … The law might be said to be a definition of the minimum acceptable standards of behaviour. However, many morally contestable issues, whether in business or elsewhere, are not explicitly covered by the law. … In one sense then, business ethics can be said to begin where the law ends. Business ethics is primarily concerned with those issues not covered by the law, or where there is no definite consensus on whether something is right or wrong.

> Extracts from: Crane, A. and Matten, D. (2010) *Business Ethics,* pp.5, 7.

Essay extract 2

It is important to emphasise here that business ethics is not synonymous with legality. There is some overlap between law and ethics, but legislation usually only regulates the lowest level of acceptable behaviour (Crane and Matten 2010). Business ethics, then, as Crane and Matten state, is mainly concerned with areas of conduct *not* specifically covered by law and that are therefore open to different interpretations, a fact that means a particular behaviour may be legal albeit viewed as unethical.

Comments on the essay extracts

In essay extract 1 the student introduces the source material by stating their own point and so indicating to the reader that they are using the paraphrase to support this. In essay extract 2 the student paraphrases selectively to emphasise the fact that ethics is not the same thing as the law. They emphasise this difference because in this part of their essay they are defining and describing what business ethics is, and so want to point out the differences between business ethics, the law and morality.

Notice how in both essay paraphrases the student does not just replace individual words, but completely rewrites and reorders the source material based on their independent understanding of the text. The students' paraphrases also convey the source ideas more simply than the original source.

Notice also that both paraphrases are shorter than the original. A paraphrase can be as long and as detailed as the original text, but will often be shorter because the points are condensed and/or the language and sentence structure are simpler. Paraphrase 1 is shorter than the original extract because the student has used it in their essay introduction as just a brief example of the importance of business ethics. Paraphrase 2 is also shorter than the original extract because although the student has included all the points from the original source, they have again used simpler language and condensed the ideas in their own way.

Six points for effective paraphrase

1 Write your paraphrase from your notes and reflection rather than straight from the original text

If you have approached your reading in a similar way to that suggested in Part A, you will already be well on the way to writing good paraphrases. Using your own words will be much easier if you have gone through the process of making good notes and writing critical reflections on your reading. Remember that your paraphrase should be your own understanding and rewriting of short sections of a source, not a translation straight from the source text.

2 Use your own words and writing style

When you paraphrase you must use your own words as far as possible. The rules of academic writing do not allow you to change only a few words or even only half of the words from the original text, as this would mean you were still using a significant amount of the source unchanged. You must either change nothing and use the source as a quotation, or rewrite the source almost completely as paraphrase, with around 90 per cent of your own wording. The pattern and structure of your sentences should also be your own as far as possible.

Keeping words from the original text

There will be some words or short phrases you can't change; in the example paraphrases these words are *business ethics*, *ethical market*, *law* and *behaviour*. You do not need to put quotation marks around such commonly used words, unless the author has used a word in a unique or special way (see p.58). You should also try to rephrase statistics. For example, *one-fifth* can also be expressed as *20%*, and *more than double* can be expressed as *over twice as many / much*. It may not always be possible or make sense to rephrase numbers and statistics, but you should do so if you can.

3 Check that your paraphrase clearly supports the point *you* are making

Don't let your paraphrases take control of your essay. Decide what point you want to make first, and then paraphrase a point from a relevant source to exemplify and/or support what you have said. You will need to use appropriate reporting verbs (e.g. *show*, *suggest*, *claim*) according to what the source text is doing and also to show what you think about it (see Chapter C1, pp.97–100).

4 Show your reader why and how you are using the paraphrase

Make sure you introduce and/or comment on the paraphrase to show your reader how it links to and supports your own point.

5 Always use an in-text reference

Using in-text references with your paraphrases is essential, not optional. In academic writing, if something is not referenced it is assumed to be both your own words *and* your own idea. You must therefore *always* give an in-text reference when paraphrasing because the ideas and information you have restated are not yours, even though you have used your own words. Not giving an in-text reference for paraphrases is the most common cause of accidental student plagiarism.

   Giving in-text references is also an important way of getting marks. Your references will show your tutor that you have done some reading and that you have understood it. Finally, by helping to make clear where you have used source material, in-text references also show your tutor (and yourself) how your reading has helped you to develop your own ideas.

6 Use reference reminder phrases

Giving an in-text reference at the start of your paraphrase will often not be enough. If your paraphrase is more than one sentence long you will usually need to make clear to your reader that the subsequent sentences are also a paraphrase rather than your own ideas. You can see that in essay extract 2 on p.62, the student has used the phrase *as Crane and Matten state* to show the reader that the sentence is a continuation of paraphrased source material.

   As a second example of using reference reminder phrases, below is a section from the student business ethics essay on p.173 in which the student paraphrases Carr. The student has used the reference reminder phrase *he suggests that* to make clear that the ideas in the second sentence are also those of Carr. If this phrase had not been used in the essay extract, the tutor would probably assume that the idea in the second sentence was the student's own.

> Carr (1968) uses the analogy of a poker game to argue that a successful businessman needs to play by the rules of the industry and that these include 'bluffing' as an acceptable form of behaviour. He suggests that what is in effect lying is merely part of legitimate business strategy, and that business rules do not need to take account of personal or social principles.

   If you don't use reference reminder phrases, it may become unclear in your essay which of your sentences express your own ideas and which ones express the ideas of other authors. This lack of clarity could lead to you plagiarising accidentally because, as stated above, in academic writing it is always assumed that any sentence without a reference is the author's (your) own comment or idea.

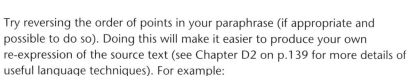

Top tip for effective paraphrasing

Try reversing the order of points in your paraphrase (if appropriate and possible to do so). Doing this will make it easier to produce your own re-expression of the source text (see Chapter D2 on p.139 for more details of useful language techniques). For example:

Source text	Student paraphrase
Both quantity and quality of sleep warrant consideration, as each has serious health implications. Both characteristics are correlates of diseases such as overall health and specific illnesses such as coronary heart disease; individually, sleep duration has been linked to obesity and impaired neurobehavioral performance, and sleep quality has ties to depression. Extract from: Chiou, J. H. et al. (2016) 'Correlates of self-report chronic insomnia disorders with 1–6 month and 6-month durations in home-dwelling urban older adults – the Shih-Pai Sleep Study in Taiwan: a cross-sectional community study', *BMC Geriatrics* 16, p.119.	Chiou et al. (2016) and others have shown that poor sleep has been linked to depression, and a lack of sleep to poor brain function and obesity. Moreover, these studies show that both aspects of sleep have an impact on specific diseases (e.g. heart disease) and on general health, and that it is therefore important to investigate both sleep quality and quantity.

How much of your essay should consist of paraphrase?

This will depend on many factors, including your subject, assignment type and title. If you are conducting your own experiment or research you may not be using many sources and therefore not be paraphrasing. However, most types of undergraduate essay will consist of quite a few short paraphrases (some of which will be summaries) of different source texts. If you look at academic journal articles in your subject, you will see that some of them have up to half of their content in the form of paraphrase, often from many different sources and therefore with many different in-text references. The business ethics essay on pp.173–178 has about half of its word count as paraphrase and summary, but is still original because of the student's choice of sources and how they have used and evaluated them.

The thing to avoid is having lots of short paraphrases and summaries that are merely stitched together with only a few phrases and sentences of your own. You might inadvertently fall into this trap if you don't emphasise your own points or develop your own argument enough, or if you don't comment on your paraphrases, showing how they support your viewpoint. If you find yourself just stitching things together, go back and do some more thinking about what your own argument is. Then try to emphasise this more in your writing, summarise and group your sources more, and give more of your own evaluations and comments to show your reader how your sources support your own points.

Four common paraphrasing errors

- **not showing clearly the switches between your own points and paraphrase**

You must make clear to your reader which are your words and ideas and which sentences are paraphrased. For example, if you only give one in-text reference in brackets at the end of a long paragraph, it won't be clear which sentences in that paragraph are paraphrase and which are your own points. Every switch between you and your sources must be clear.

As an example of this, below is an annotated student essay extract.

Showing the switches

	No reference, which tells the reader that the first sentence is the student's own point
Business ethics is not the same thing as either legality or general morality. Crane and Matten (2010) point out that there is some overlap between law and ethics, but legislation usually only regulates the lowest level of acceptable behaviour. They also state that this necessitates a whole range of other principles and guidelines to encourage businesses to rise above the most basic level of conduct. Legislation is crucial in forcing businesses to behave well, and needs to be kept under constant review.	Reference, indicating to the reader that this second sentence is a switch from student to source
	Reference reminder phrase, indicating to the reader that this third sentence is not a switch between student and source, but a continuation of the paraphrase
	No reference, which tells the reader that this fourth sentence is a switch back to the student's own points

● **Not making enough changes from the original source**

Students sometimes use just a few of their own words to stitch together unchanged sentences or phrases from a source or from several different sources. Even if you give the relevant in-text references, this type of writing constitutes plagiarism because most of the words and style are not your own.

● **Changing individual words but keeping the same sentence pattern as the original**

This might happen if you don't make notes and reflect on your reading but just try to 'translate' word by word from the text straight into your essay. Even if you change all the words, your paraphrase will still have the same style and pattern of the original text, and is therefore still a type of plagiarism.

● **Accidentally changing the meaning of the original text**

This might happen if you have not read and understood the text carefully enough, not reflected on it, or have not made clear notes. Make sure you understand from the text what is fact and what is opinion, and pay particular attention to small but important words such as *no, not* or *not as* (see Chapter A2, pp.21–24).

Examples of poor paraphrases

Below is a short extract from a journal article that looks at whether mobile phones are a health risk. The extract is followed by three poor paraphrases which all try to use this article to support the view that mobile phones do not damage health.

Read the extract and then read and evaluate each paraphrase before reading the comments.

Source extract

So far there is no clear evidence from health studies of a relation between mobile phone use and mortality or morbidity. Indeed, tantalising findings in humans include a speeding up of reaction time during exposure, particularly during behavioural tasks calling for attention and electrical brain activity changes during cognitive processes. It is not clear, however, whether these findings have any positive implications for health.

Adapted from: Maier, M., Blakemore, C. and Koivisto, M. (2000) 'The Health Hazards of Mobile Phones', *British Medical Journal* 320(7245), pp.1288–1289.

Poor paraphrase 1

Maier et al. (2000) show that there is no clear evidence from health studies of a relation between mobile phone use and mortality or morbidity. They state that, in fact, tantalising findings in humans include a speeding up of reaction time during exposure, particularly during behavioural tasks calling for attention and changes in brain electricity during cognitive processes. It is not clear, however, whether these findings have any positive implications for health.

Comments

The student has correctly used an in-text reference and the reference reminder phrase *They state that.* However, the only changes they have made from the source are to put in these references, take off the first two words and reword the phrase 'electrical brain activity changes'. Everything else is copied word for word from the source without any use of quotation marks. This is plagiarism.

Poor paraphrase 2

Some studies point to interesting results which suggest that while using a phone, the user has quicker reaction times to some behavioural tasks (Maier et al. 2000). In fact, there are interesting findings in humans that show a speeding up of reaction time during exposure, particularly during behavioural tasks calling for attention and changes in brain electricity during cognitive processes. It is unclear whether these findings have any positive implications for health.

Comments

The student has used an in-text reference and has also made some significant changes in wording. However, there are two problems with this paraphrase. The first is that there are still several long phrases and a whole line unchanged from the original source – this could be seen as plagiarism. Secondly, there is no reference reminder phrase and so the reader is not sure whether the information in the second sentence comes from Maier et al. or from the student. Similarly, in the third sentence, it could easily be assumed that the point expressed is that of the student, and this could therefore also be seen as plagiarism.

Poor paraphrase 3

Maier et al. (2000) show that up to now there is not any strong proof from studies on disease, of a link between the use of mobile phones and death or disease. In fact, interesting results in humans include a faster time of reaction during use, especially while doing practical tasks that need concentration and brain electricity change during the thought process. It is unclear whether these results imply any health benefits (ibid.)

et al. = and the other authors
ibid. = from the same source as previously mentioned

Comments

The student has used nearly all their own words and has used two in-text references, which is good. However, they have been too dependent on the source and instead of making and using notes have gone straight from reading the article to writing the paraphrase, translating the original text word by word. The result is a paraphrase that has exactly the same 'pattern' as the original. This does not show a clear understanding of the original text and is a type of plagiarism.

An example of a good paraphrase

Below is an acceptable paraphrase of the Maier et al. (2000) extract.

> Studies point to interesting results suggesting that mobile phone users experience quicker reaction times to tasks which require both changes in electrical brain activity and concentration (Maier et al. 2000). Although it has not been shown that this effect represents an actual benefit to health, there have equally been no data from any disease studies to suggest that mobile phones actually damage health in any way (ibid.).

Over to You 10
What do you think of these paraphrases?

Below is a short extract from a different article on the issue of mobile phones and health risks. Below the extract are four poor paraphrases. Read the extract and then the paraphrases and identify what is wrong with each one. Comments and also two examples of acceptable paraphrases of the extract can be found on p.183, one using author/date referencing and the other a numeric referencing.

Source extract

Mobile phones provide an interesting example of a source risk to health which may be largely non-existent but which cannot be totally dismissed. Such risks, when possibly serious and with long-term consequences, are typically dealt with by appeal to the so-called precautionary principle but, of course, precaution comes at a price.

Extract from: Cox, D. R. (2003), 'Communication of risk: health hazards from mobile phones', *Journal of the Royal Statistical Society: Series A (Statistics in Society)* 166(2), pp.214–246.

Poor paraphrases

1   Advising caution in the use of mobile phones is an example of a typical approach to the fear of a possible health risk which may be of a serious nature. Such an approach may have negative consequences, but is taken because although there may in fact be no health risk, this has not yet been proven.

2   Cox (2003) suggests that advising caution in the use of mobile phones is an example of a typical approach to the fear of a possible health risk which may be of a serious nature. Such an approach may have negative consequences, but is taken because although there may in fact be no health risk, this has not yet been proven.

3   Advising caution in the use of mobile phones is an example of a typical approach to the fear of a possible health risk which may be of a serious nature. Such an approach may have negative consequences but is taken because although there may in fact be no health risk, this has not yet been proven (Cox 2003).

4   Mobile phones provide an interesting example of a source risk to health which may be largely non-existent but which cannot be totally dismissed (Cox 2003). So far there is no clear evidence from health studies of a relation between mobile phone use and mortality or morbidity.

Over to You 11
Write a paraphrase

Paraphrase the source extract below. An example of a good paraphrase can be found on p.184.

Source extract

Extensive evidence reviews have been conducted to understand possible carcinogenic risks posed by mobile radiation. Overall, the results have detracted from the hypothesis that mobile phone use affects the occurrence of intracranial tumors, and in addition, no evidence of an association between general tumor risk and cellular telephone use among either short-term or long-term users was found.

Adapted extract from: Verma, A., Kohli, C. and Ingle, G. K. (2016) 'Mobile Phone Use and Possible Cancer Risk: Current Perspectives in India', *Indian Journal of Occupational and Environmental Medicine* 20(1), pp.5–9.

Summary

- Re-expressing source material in your own words and style is a key part of academic writing, and a powerful way of building on the ideas of others to develop your own argument.

- Make sure you introduce and/or comment on your paraphrase to show your reader why and how you are using it to help develop your own argument.

- You must use about 90 per cent or more of your own words and sentence patterns – a 50/50 per cent approach is not acceptable.

- In your paraphrase the words, style and sentence pattern are your own but the ideas are not, so always use an in-text reference.

- Use in-text referencing and reference reminder phrases to make clear where all the switches are between you and your source material, and remember that if a sentence has no reference it is assumed to be your own point.

- Paraphrasing is a complex skill and takes time to do well – you will get better at it the more you practise.

B3

Why and how should you summarise?

Summarising a text means reporting its main points in your own way, using your own words and style. Summarising is a type of paraphrasing, but the term *paraphrase* is commonly used to refer to the process of re-expressing a specific point contained in a short piece of source text, whereas a summary gives only the main points from a much larger section or from the whole text.

Why summarise?

Summarising is a common and effective way of using source material, and is a key element in essays and other types of assignment. Summarising what an author says allows you to:

➤ show your tutor that you have understood what you have read;
➤ express the information and ideas from sources in your own style of thinking and writing so that you can integrate them smoothly into your argument and essay;
➤ restate information and ideas from sources in a way that best supports your own argument;
➤ show how you have used sources to develop your knowledge and ideas;
➤ express information and ideas from complicated texts more clearly and simply.

   A source summary is a very powerful way of using source material because it allows you to show that you have understood the key point of a text and that you can express it in your own way. You will need to summarise in order to synthesise your sources – to compare, connect and group sources in relation to your own points (see Chapters A4 and A5). Importantly, you should never put a source summary into your essay without introducing and/or commenting on it to show the reader why you are using it as part of the development of your own argument.

How long should a source summary be?

The length and level of detail of your summary will depend on what you want it to do in your essay. A summary that includes all the main points of a text may be up to a third as long as the original. Often, however, you will want to give just a brief summary, perhaps of only a few sentences or even just one phrase, to express the key point of the text.

Some examples of very short summaries

Below are two separate extracts from the business ethics essay on pp.173–178. Read each extract and think about why and how the student has briefly summarised their sources (in shaded light blue) before reading the comment on each extract.

Essay extract 1

Opponents of the concept of ethics in business include those who claim that making a profit is the only responsibility a business has to society (Friedman 1970, cited in Fisher and Lovell 2003). Others such as Wolf (2008) share this view, and Carr (1968) uses the analogy of a poker game to argue that a successful businessman needs to play by the rules of the industry and that these include 'bluffing' as an acceptable form of behaviour. He suggests that what is in effect lying is merely part of legitimate business strategy, and that business rules do not need to take account of personal or social principles.

Comment

In the first part of the first sentence the student both introduces their sources and shows the reader that they are about to summarise sources that oppose the idea of business ethics. The student then summarises the viewpoint of Friedman in one sentence, and then in effect briefly summarises the overall position of Wolf in only four words by stating 'Wolf shares this view.' The student then links Wolf to Carr and gives a summary of Carr's poker analogy. In the final sentence the student summarises Carr's overall position.

Essay extract 2

As I stated earlier, importantly, the four reasons I give above for the relevance of business ethics all stem from the fact that organisations and society are interdependent. This idea is supported by Shaw and Barry (2007), Green (1994), Fritzsche (2005), Svensson and Wood (2008) and others. Svensson and Wood (2008) offer a model that shows how business and society are mutually dependent and responsible for the consequences and effects of the other in a continuous and dynamic process. Importantly, they suggest that not only are the ethical standards of business connected to those of society, they actually stem from them. I would add that …

Comment

In the first sentence the student states their own point. They then link, summarise and group four different sources, showing that they understand the key point of all of these texts and also understand that these authors all hold a similar position on the issue. The student then expands their summary of Svensson and Wood because this source gives an important point that supports their position.

Six steps for writing good summaries

Step 1 Identify how the source text is organised

Writing a good summary starts with your reading. Make sure you understand how the text is structured. Read the title, sub-headings, introduction and conclusion of the text to help you identify the key points. Identify which parts of the text are main points and which are examples of these points or more minor points.

Step 2 Understand, make clear notes and critically reflect on your reading

If you have approached your reading in a similar way to the steps given in Part A, you will already be well on the way to writing effective summaries. If you have written an annotated bibliography entry and a critical reflection on a text, these will probably already contain your own summary which you can then improve and modify for use in your essay.

Step 3 Summarise what the text is about in one or two sentences

A useful exercise is to use your notes to write a very short summary in only one or two sentences. Doing this helps you to clarify in your mind the key message of the text. If you need to you can then write a longer, more detailed summary.

Step 4 Think about why and how you want to use the summary

Before you put your summary into your essay, ask yourself how it fits into your overall essay plan and argument.

Step 5 Show your reader why and how you are using the summary

Make sure you introduce and/or comment on each summary to show your reader how it links to and supports your own point.

Step 6 Check that you have used your own words and style, in-text references and reference reminder phrases

Check that you have written your summary using your own words as far as possible and that you have used adequate in-text referencing. If your summary is more than one sentence long you will also need to use a reference reminder phrase (see Chapter B2, p.64).

Five common mistakes students make when summarising:

➢ accidentally changing the meaning of the original text;
➢ giving too much detail and putting in minor points, examples or definitions from the text rather than just the main points;

➢ adding their own comments within the summary, making it hard for the reader to distinguish between the two;

➢ not making enough changes in words and style from the original source;

➢ not making clear where the summary begins and ends (i.e. not using clear in-text references and reference reminder phrases).

Over to You 12
What's wrong with these summaries?

Below is a text extract. Read it and make your own notes and then write a short summary. Next read and evaluate the four summaries and read the comments on each one. Finally, have a look at the two good summaries.

A study on links between emotion regulation, job satisfaction and intentions to quit

Côté and Morgan (2002) conducted a study that looks at the relationship between emotion regulation, job satisfaction and intention to quit one's job. They collected two sets of data from 111 workers. The participants gave informed consent and were asked to complete two questionnaires on how they felt they had regulated their emotions at work and their feelings about their job. There was a time interval of four weeks between the two questionnaires to allow enough time for changes in emotion regulation but also to have a short enough period to maintain the retention of the participants.

Côté and Morgan showed from their data that the amplification of pleasant emotions happened more frequently than the suppression of unpleasant emotions. Importantly, they also found a strong correlation between emotion regulation and job satisfaction and intention to quit. They demonstrated that, as they predicted, the suppression of unpleasant emotions leads to a decrease in job satisfaction and therefore an increase in intention to quit. Their findings also suggest that an increase in the amplification of pleasant emotions will increase job satisfaction, because it increases positive social interaction and more positive responses from colleagues and customers.

Although their experiment showed that emotion regulation affects job satisfaction, there was no strong evidence to suggest a reverse correlation i.e. that job satisfaction and intention to quit influence emotional regulation.

Source: Robinson, J. (2011) 'A study on links between emotion regulation, job satisfaction and intentions to quit', *Business Reports that Matter* 3, p.41.

Poor summary 1

Côté and Morgan (2002) have conducted a study that looks at the relationship between emotion regulation, job satisfaction and intention to quit one's job. Côté and Morgan showed from their data that the amplification of pleasant emotions happened more frequently than the suppression of unpleasant emotions. Importantly, they also found a strong correlation between emotion regulation and job satisfaction and intention to quit.

Comments

This summary consists of four sentences copied word for word from the original text. This is therefore plagiarism. In addition to this, the student has only given an in-text reference for Côté and Morgan, which implies that they have read this primary article, when in fact they have only read the Robinson text. This is a form of plagiarism.

Poor summary 2

A study has shown a strong link between emotion regulation and job satisfaction and intention to quit (Côté and Morgan 2002, cited in Robinson, 2011). An example of emotion regulation is when someone attempts to hide the anger they feel towards their boss or when they pretend to be happier than they really are during a work meeting or when dealing with customers. Côté and Morgan tested 111 workers by asking them to complete two questionnaires at an interval of four weeks. They found that workers exaggerate positive emotions more than they hide negative feelings. The findings also showed that suppressing negative feelings leads to lower job satisfaction and that amplifying positive feelings leads to better work relationships and therefore higher job satisfaction.

Comments

The first and the last two sentences of this summary are good, with correct in-text references. However, in the middle of the summary the student has included different examples of what emotion regulation is and also details of the method of the study, neither of which should be in a summary.

Poor summary 3

Robinson (2011) describes a study conducted by Côté and Morgan, in which they obtained data on emotion regulation from 111 workers. The findings suggest that workers exaggerate positive emotions more than they hide negative feelings and that there is strong evidence that how you feel about your job influences how you regulate your emotions at work.

Comments

Summary 3 starts with a correct in-text reference and the summary is written in the student's own words and style, which is good. However, the last point in the summary is not correct – the study showed that emotion regulation can influence how you feel about your job, but that there was *no* evidence that job satisfaction affects emotion regulation.

Poor summary 4

A study has shown a strong link between emotion regulation and job satisfaction and intention to quit (Côté and Morgan 2002, cited in Robinson, 2011) and that workers exaggerate positive emotions more than they hide negative feelings. This might be because workers are worried that if they show their negative feelings, they might not get promoted, or worse, that they may lose their job. The findings also showed that suppressing negative feelings leads to a decrease in job satisfaction and a corresponding increase in wanting to leave, and that amplifying positive feelings leads to more positive interaction at work and therefore more job satisfaction.

Comments

This summary starts and ends well, with a clear statement of the key point and correct in-text references. However, the second sentence is the student's own idea of why workers might hide negative feelings, and this should not be part of the summary. Any comments or opinion by the student on the results of the Côté and Morgan study should come after the summary rather than within it, so that it is clear to the reader which is summary and which is student comment.

A good one-sentence summary

A study has shown a strong link between regulating emotions at work and job satisfaction levels, and therefore intention to quit (Côté and Morgan 2002, cited in Robinson 2011).

A good three-sentence summary

A study has shown that people exaggerate positive emotions more than they hide negative feelings when at work (Côté and Morgan 2002, cited in Robinson 2011). Côté and Morgan established a strong link between regulating emotions, job satisfaction and intention to quit. They found that suppressing negative feelings leads to lower levels of job satisfaction, and that amplifying positive feelings leads to better relationships at work and therefore more job satisfaction. However, they found no evidence of job satisfaction level affecting how people regulate their emotions at work.

Over to You 13
Write a summary

Read and make notes on the text below. From your notes, write a one-sentence and then a two- or three-sentence summary. Each summary should include an in-text reference and reference reminder phrase. Compare your summaries with the examples given on p.184.

Source text

Sport in the UK: the role of the DCMS

The Department for Culture, Media and Sport (DCMS) is responsible for delivering Government policy on sport, from supporting the performance and preparation of elite individual performers and teams to increasing sporting opportunities at all levels, but especially for the young, to encourage long-lasting participation.

DCMS recognizes that success in sport by UK representatives at the elite level, such as athletes at the Olympics or football teams in European competition, can enhance the reputation of the country and make large numbers of people feel proud. To that end, it provides funding where it will make a difference, such as through the Talented Athlete Scholarship Scheme, and political support where that is more suitable, such as to the Football Association's attempts to be awarded the right to host the 2018 FIFA World Cup in England.

DCMS also supports opportunities to participate in sport in schools and communities, regardless of the level of performance. Among DCMS' targets are that by 2008, 85% of 5–16-year-olds will be taking physical education and other school sports for a minimum of two hours per week, and that by 2012 all children will have the opportunity of at least four hours of weekly sport (DCMS 2008).

Widening participation will help to identify the next generation of potential elite performers at an early stage, but DCMS also has other less obvious goals in mind. They claim that continued participation in sport from an early age will lead to a more active population and that this will help to address the problem of increasing levels and frequency of obesity and so reduce the risk of coronary heart disease, stroke, type 2 diabetes and certain types of cancer. Clearly, the benefits of sport to the nation are not simply about medal tables and championships.

Source: Dobson, C. (2010) *Sport and the Nation.*

Summary

● Express only the main point or points from the original text.
● Don't include your own comments or evaluation of the sources inside the summary.

- Do comment before and/or after the summary to show your reader why you have used it.

- Your summary should be your own expression, style and words as far as possible. It is not acceptable to change only a few words of the original text or to sew together unchanged sentences from different parts of the source.

- If your summary is more than one sentence long, check whether you need to use reference reminder phrases to make clear to your reader that the later sentences are also points from your source.

- Always give an in-text reference with your summary, as the ideas are not your own, even though the words are. Summarising without giving an in-text reference is a form of plagiarism.

What will make your essay original?

The originality of your essay will depend not just on which sources or how many you use, but on how and why you use them. Two essays addressing the same title and using the same sources can still differ greatly because of the way each one has used the source material to develop and reach a unique perspective and conclusion.

Your essay will be original if you:

- understand your source texts accurately so that you can analyse, question and evaluate them properly (see Chapter A2);
- compare and connect your sources in your own way to reveal new relationships and patterns (see Chapter A4);
- use your source synthesis to reach your own new way of seeing the issue, your own conclusions and your own further questions (see Chapter A5, p.46 and Chapter B5);
- re-express and integrate your sources accurately into your essay using your own words and style to develop your own argument (see Chapters B2 and B3);
- make clear to your reader whether each sentence in your essay is expressing your own point or that of source authors (see Chapters B2 and B3).

Your essay might lack originality and/or contain accidental plagiarism if you:

- don't understand, analyse or evaluate your source properly;
- cut and paste different bits of different sources together or give 'lists' of source summaries or paraphrases rather than comparing, grouping and synthesising your material;
- use source material without explicitly introducing or commenting on it to show your reader why you are using it;
- when paraphrasing, mix your words with those of your sources (a 'half and half' approach) rather than using about 90 per cent of your own words and style;
- use source material without sufficient in-text references and reference reminder phrases;
- use too many quotations sewn together in an uncritical manner.

What does 'presenting an argument' mean?

Developing and presenting an argument means using a series of logical steps that you support with evidence to reach a persuasive conclusion. 'Arguing' in this sense does not necessarily mean that you have to disagree with someone or something, although in order to develop a strong argument you will need to address the whole range of views on the topic, some of which will differ from your own.

Can you give your opinion in an essay?

You might think or be told not to give opinions in academic assignments. What tutors mean by this is that you should not give opinions in the sense of judgements or impressions based only on feelings, preferences and/or personal experience. What you *are* expected to do, particularly in discursive essays, is to present views you have formed as a result of evidenced reasoning (i.e. through argument, as described above). Indeed, the best academic work is transformative, meaning that an analysis and synthesis of evidence has led the writer to clarify, modify or change their previously held position. So, the type of phrases your tutors do *not* want to see in your essays are:

> ➢ I think/feel that it is wrong to use animals to make clothes because I think animals have feelings and shouldn't be used like this.
> ➢ These large-scale studies suggest that homeopathy is not effective, but I still feel that it works.
> ➢ I believe in the power of the mind.
> ➢ I prefer towns to cities.

The type of things your tutors do want to see are:

> ➢ I will argue that using leather clothing is wrong because … and I will use four key pieces of evidence to support my position. Firstly, …
> ➢ These large-scale studies suggest that homeopathy is not effective. Therefore, any instinctive, personal views that it does work should be disregarded, as the current evidence indicates otherwise.

Giving enough time to the 'using sources' process

A common cause of lack of originality and accidental plagiarism in assignments is that the student writer has not been able to give enough time to each stage of the process, particularly the early stages of understanding and becoming familiar with their source material.

Figure 7 below gives approximate minimum times needed for searching online and then using four academic journal articles in an essay. In reality the time needed will, of course, vary according to each individual student and the source and assignment type, but it is still useful to have some rough guidelines you can use to help you plan your time. Notice that 'thinking time' is important both within and between each stage.

Thinking	Stage	Thinking	Time
Thinking	Finding and selecting four relevant texts; Writing a research log entry for each text	Thinking	1–2 hours
Thinking	Reading, questioning, evaluating and locating each text in the subject	Thinking	4 hours
Thinking	Re-reading each text and making clear and meaningful notes	Thinking	2–3 hours
Thinking	Writing a critical reflection from your notes on each text that includes whether/how it has developed or changed your viewpoint	Thinking	1 hour
Thinking	Comparing and connecting the four texts and using the resulting insights to develop your own ideas	Thinking	1 hour
Thinking	Deciding why and how you want to use the texts in your draft essay to support your argument	Thinking	1 hour
Thinking	Integrating ideas or information from the texts into your draft essay as paraphrase, summary or quotation	Thinking	2 hours
Thinking	Checking that your sources precisely support your points, that when paraphrasing you have used your own words and style, and that you have used in-text references and reference reminder phrases		1 hour

Total of 13–15 hours

Figure 7 Rough time guidelines for using four journal articles or book chapters in your essay

Review of the whole process from source selection to final essay

In Parts A and B of this book we have often used two texts to illustrate the main stages in the process of using source material. These texts are Svensson and Wood (2008), 'A model of business ethics' and Carr (1968), 'Is business bluffing ethical?' Below is a brief reminder of the process the student writer went through in using the Svensson and Wood article.

● **Deciding to read the Svensson and Wood (2008) article (p.15)**

As an example of thinking about source types before searching for material, the student decided to look first for textbooks that would give definitions of business ethics. They also realised that they would need some relevant journal articles by key authors for views on the importance of business ethics …

● **Reading the article (p.31)**

> … it is important to see business ethics as a highly dynamic and continuous process without an end. A process, however, that is predicated on the interrelationship between business and society where each one is interdependent and responsible together for the outcomes …
>
> Svensson, G. and Wood, G. (2008) 'A Model of Business Ethics',
> *Journal of Business Ethics* 77, pp.303–322.

● **Making notes on the article (pp.41–42)**

> p.319 main point   BE – '… dynamic and continuous process …' –
>   'interrelationship between businesses and society'
>   – each responsible for the other.

● **Writing a critical analysis and reflection of the article (p.31)**

> *The authors offer a model to show that managers should act ethically because they are intrinsically part of society. They look only at businesses operating in a developed world and a capitalist context, and presumably there are lots of businesses outside these types of context, but they don't mention these …*

- **Comparing and connecting sources using a synthesis diagram (pp.37 and 81)**

Figure 8   Comparing and connecting sources using a synthesis diagram

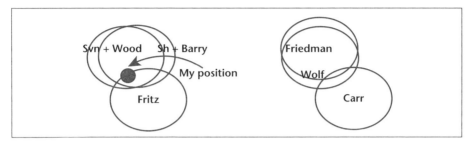

- **Making source synthesis notes (p.45)**

Figure 9   Whether businesses should/have to behave ethically

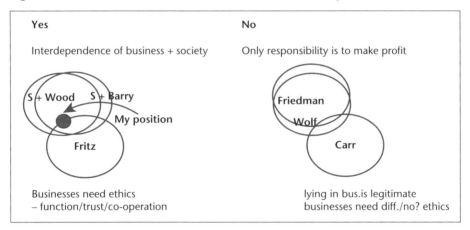

- **Writing a source synthesis reflection (p.46)**

Svensson and Wood take a similar position to that of Esty, Collins, Shaw and Barry and on the opposite side to Freidman, Wolf and Carr. The article puts forward a theoretical model which they say has not been done before and that it is therefore doing something new, i.e. filling a gap in theory. They expect other academics to argue or disagree with their model of business ethics. The main message of their article is very similar to that of Shaw and Barry ...

● **Integrating the Svensson and Wood article into the final essay (p.176)**

As I have stated, the four reasons I give for the relevance of business ethics all stem from the fact that organisations and society are interdependent. This idea is supported by Shaw and Barry (2007), Green (1994), Fritzsche (2005), Svensson and Wood (2008) and others. Svensson and Wood offer a model showing how business and society are mutually dependent and responsible for the consequences and effects of the other in a continuous and dynamic process. I would say that a practical manifestation of this idea is the fact that ...

Summary

- Try to plan your study so that you can give enough time to each stage of the 'using source' process: selection, understanding, analysis, evaluation and synthesis.
- Integrate your source material correctly into your essay via good paraphrasing and in-text referencing.
- Present an evidenced argument and informed views rather than personal opinions.
- Doing all of the above will result in an interesting and original essay.

B5

Putting it all together in your essay

This final chapter in Part B looks at examples of synthesising source material clearly and successfully to produce a finished essay.

Figure 10   Using your reading in your essay

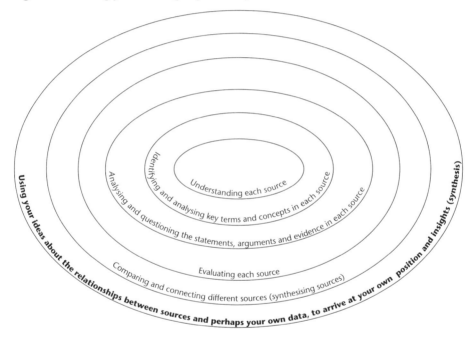

Below are two annotated and colour-coded paragraphs from the business ethics essay on pp.173–178, showing two points in the assignment where the student writer has synthesised their source material with their own points and argument. As you read the essay extracts note that:

> the paragraphs have a sequence of either black – shaded light-blue, or black – shaded light-blue – black, indicating the pattern of student point followed by sources used as support and then usually a further student comment;

> the sources are integrated using paraphrase and summary rather than quotation;

> the student uses more than one source to support a particular point;

➤ the student has grouped their sources;

➤ every sentence that conveys ideas from source material has either some form of reference to the author or reference reminder phrase (in dark blue).

Paragraphs from the business ethics essay

Views differ widely about whether ethics have a valid place in business, from a clear 'yes', and the argument that ethical behaviour should be a core value in any organisation, and a definite 'no', with the argument that ethics should not play any part in a business. Opponents of the concept of ethics in business include those who claim that making a profit is the only responsibility a business has to society (Friedman 1970, cited in Fisher and Lovell 2003). Others such as Wolf (2008) share this view, and Carr (1968) uses the analogy of a poker game to argue that ... Similarly, Prindl and Prodham (1994) point out that 'Finance as practised in the professions and in industry is seen as a value-neutral positive discipline, promoting efficiency without regard to the social consequences which follow from its products' (p. 3).	Student point Source material synthesised and integrated to support the student's point
A consideration of the impact on the outward-facing aspects of a business bring us to the second reason I give for the need of organisations to behave in an ethical manner, that of market growth and profit. ... It is becoming more frequently the case that 'citizens of first world societies expect their corporations to display integrity in their international business dealings' (Svensson and Wood 2008 p. 312), and Trevino and Nelson (2010) state that a perception that an organisation is behaving well will increase its attractiveness and thereby its stakeholder commitment. Esty (2007) also notes that companies are now expected to publish reports on aspects of their activities such as greenhouse gas emission and energy performance, and if they do not reach expected ethical targets, their reputation and possibly also their financial investment prospects are likely to suffer – a point that links back to the idea of businesses actually needing to be ethical to be profitable.	Student point Sources synthesised and integrated to support the student's point Student point

Finally, below are the two points in the essay conclusion where the student explains to the reader the two new insights they have arrived at through their analysis and synthesis of sources. Importantly, note firstly that by providing these insights, the student writer also goes beyond the basic essay question, and secondly that providing a new perspective is, in effect, creating a new piece of knowledge in the field.

Extracts from the essay conclusion	
Importantly, I have argued that it is imperative for an organisation to behave well for four overlapping reasons – functional need, marketing need, regulatory need and moral imperative, and that these, together with related study of, and training in, business ethics, are all different manifestations of the same fact; that businesses are an integral part of society.	Student's first new insight
Finally, I would go further than saying that business ethics is important, and suggest that it is now essential, due to aspects of globalisation such as social media and other forms of information-sharing and consumer power that have greatly increased social and businesses interconnectedness, and that therefore organisations who want to operate successfully in today's global marketplace both need and are obliged to uphold and display ethical behaviour. … Thus I would suggest that the views of those such as Carr, Friedman and Wolf are doubly wrong, because not only have businesses always been part of society and therefore beholden to play by its rules, but that all parts of society are now even more interconnected in today's technological world.	Student's second new insight

You can read the complete business ethics essay on pp.173–178, and see how the student writer uses their reading to develop their argument as the essay progresses to reach the conclusions and insights above.

Top tip for an effective essay

When you have written your essay, print it out and read through it as an objective, outside reader. Note down the main point of each paragraph and then read your notes to see whether the essay has a logical and strong argument, whether some points need rearranging or deleting, and whether points need to be added to make the argument and final concluding insights logical, persuasive and clear.

Over to You 14
What do you think of the way the source text has been used in these essay paragraphs?

Below are three paragraphs from three separate essays addressing the title: 'In what ways might personality affect job satisfaction?'

All three students have used the Robinson text on p.76. Re-read the original Robinson text and then read each essay paragraph and decide how well you think each student has used the source material. Then read the commentaries and finally, the example of an acceptable paragraph.

Poor paragraph 1

There does seem to be a link between personality and job satisfaction. One interesting study on emotion regulation has demonstrated that there is a strong link between how we regulate our emotions at work and how satisfied we are with our jobs (Côté and Morgan 2002, cited in Robinson 2011). Their data showed that the amplification of pleasant emotions happened more frequently than the suppression of unpleasant emotions. Importantly, they also found a strong correlation between emotion regulation and job satisfaction and intention to quit. I would argue that Côté and Morgan's research suggests that if you are someone who can channel negative feelings to use them in a constructive way at work in order to find a solution to the problem, you will probably have higher job satisfaction than someone who hides negative emotions without trying to resolve them.

Comments

This paragraph starts well, with the student introducing their own point that there is a link between personality and job satisfaction. They then start to paraphrase the Robinson article and give a correct in-text reference. However, the third and fourth sentences are copied word for word from the Robinson text without any quotation marks; this is plagiarism. The paragraph ends with the student's own comment, which is a good thing, but it is a different point to the one they introduce in the first sentence.

Poor paragraph 2

There does seem to be a link between personality and job satisfaction. A study has shown that there is a strong link between how we regulate our emotions at work and how satisfied we are with our jobs. Workers exaggerate positive emotions more than they hide negative feelings. In addition, suppressing negative emotions leads to less job satisfaction and amplifying positive emotions leads to better social interaction at work and therefore more job satisfaction. Côté and Morgan's research suggests that if you are someone who can channel negative feelings to use them in a constructive way at work in order to find a solution to the problem, you will probably have higher job satisfaction than someone who hides negative emotions without trying to resolve them (Côté and Morgan 2002, cited in Robinson 2011).

Comments

The student starts well by introducing their own point. They continue by summarising the Robinson text in their own words, which is good. However, they do not give any in-text references or reference reminder phrases; this is plagiarism. After their summary they continue with their own comments on the implications of the study (Côté *and Morgan's research suggests …*) but then at the end of the last sentence they give an in-text reference which they mean to refer to the previous sentences, rather than this last one, which is their own point. Putting the reference at the end of the whole paragraph is confusing for the reader, and means that they are both misrepresenting the source and not getting credit for their own idea. Finally, the student's point in the last sentence does not directly link to the one they introduce in the first sentence.

Poor paragraph 3

Côté and Morgan claim that there is a strong link between emotion regulation and job satisfaction and intention to quit (Côté and Morgan 2002, cited in Robinson 2011). The findings showed that workers exaggerate positive emotions more than they hide negative feelings. Côté and Morgan also found that suppressing negative emotions leads to less job satisfaction and that amplifying positive emotions leads to better social interaction at work and therefore more job satisfaction.

Comments

This paragraph contains only the summary of the Robinson text. There are in-text references but there is no introduction or conclusion by the student, and we therefore have no idea what point the student is trying to make. This is an example of the sources controlling the essay – the student has merely found sources they think might be relevant and put them in, without introducing them or thinking about what point they want the sources to support.

Example of an acceptable essay paragraph

There does seem to be a link between personality and job satisfaction. One interesting study on emotion regulation has demonstrated that there is a strong link between how we regulate our emotions at work, and how satisfied we are with our jobs (Côté and Morgan 2002, cited in Robinson 2011). These findings showed that workers	Student point
	Summary of source used as evidence and support

exaggerate positive emotions more than they hide negative feelings. Importantly, Côté and Morgan also found that suppressing negative feelings in fact leads to less job satisfaction, but that amplifying positive ones leads to better social interaction at work and therefore higher job satisfaction. Established personality types, as outlined in the introduction of this essay, include a 'detached' type, where the person finds it difficult to express feelings, particularly when they are negative and when doing so might cause conflict. I would suggest therefore, that one implication of Côté and Morgan's research is that such a person is likely to have lower job satisfaction, and that conversely, a less detached employee will generally be a more satisfied worker.

| Student's idea and insight that links back to the first sentence |

How should you use your reading in reflective writing?

A reflective piece is different from other types of assignment in that you are reflecting on something you have done, rather than putting forward a persuasive argument or trying to find a solution. In a reflective assignment, therefore, you will probably want to use less source material than in a discursive essay. However, some reflective assignments require that you both reflect on your own practice and appraise it in relation to theory, and so in this case you will be using sources for the specific purpose of reflecting on this link. If and when you use and integrate sources into a reflective essay, you should do so in the same way as for other types of academic writing.

As an example of this, below is an extract from a student reflective report on the performance of their team in managing a small construction project.

Extract from a reflective report

Our team decided that in view of the limited time and the fact that we could only conduct one workshop on the specified date, we would hold an initial 'information sharing' workshop with the whole construction project team. Gathering and sharing information before starting the series of project design workshops is the first key stage in value management (Green 1994, Rains 2008, Mir and Pinnington 2014 and others). In particular, collecting information is a crucial element in deciding on cost-effective design and so avoiding more expensive changes later on (Cloete, 2008). Our workshop went well generally, but on reflection I think it would have been better to …

How should you use your reading in reports?

As with reflective essays, it is the purpose and context for your use of sources that will differ between a discursive essay and a report, rather than the mechanics of how you integrate material. The purpose of a report is usually to collect, analyse and convey specific information and then to recommend actions and/or to suggest solutions. This will probably mean that the types of source material you use in a report will be more information-driven rather than discursive or argumentative, and that there will be perhaps a little less critical evaluation of the information, and more synthesis in terms of gathering and presenting the relevant facts and information needed to then give recommendations.

If you write a report that involves conducting some of your own research, reference to other source material will usually only be appropriate in your introduction and discussion sections rather than in your methodology, method and results sections, and therefore you will use fewer sources overall as compared to a discursive essay. A final difference between essays and reports is that reports more often use a numeric style of in-text referencing rather than an author and date system (see Appendix 5, p.205).

One point to remember is that tutors often use the terms *report* and *essay* in an overlapping or even interchangeable manner, and that an assignment might in fact be a hybrid between the two genres. If you are unsure about the format or requirements for a report or an essay, ask your tutor for guidance.

As an illustration of the fact that source material is often used in a similar way in both reports and essays, particularly in the introductory and concluding sections, below is a short extract from the first chapter of the 2018 World Bank Development Report. The report uses a numeric referencing system.

Education as freedom

Since 1948, education has been recognized as a basic human right, highlighting its role as a safeguard for human dignity and a foundation of freedom, justice, and peace.[1] In the language of Amartya Sen's capability approach, education increases both an individual's assets and his or her ability to transform them into well-being—or what has been called the individual's "beings and doings" and "capabilities."[2] Education can have corresponding salutary effects on communities and societies.

Extract from: World Bank (2018) *World Development Report 2018: Learning to Realize Education's Promise*. Washington, DC: World Bank, p.38.

Summary

- In your essays your tutors want to see that you have been able to discriminate between different sources and have selected the most relevant ones.

- Get the best marks possible for your work by always giving in-text references so that your tutor can distinguish your ideas from those of your sources. Referencing all your sources also makes your work more credible and therefore more persuasive.

- An effective use of quotation, paraphrase and summary will enable you to control your sources and make them work for you in your essay.

- Never use a source without commenting on it in some way.

- Even if you use a lot of source material, your essay will still be original because of which sources you have used, how you have analysed and evaluated them, and how you have used them to develop and support your argument and your individual answer to the assignment question.

Part C

Useful words and phrases

C1

Using verbs precisely and powerfully

Parts A and B of this book have looked at the different ways you can write about and integrate your reading into your essays, including how to show clearly the difference between your ideas and those of your sources. Using verbs in an appropriate and precise way is essential for doing these things effectively, and this chapter gives you information and examples to help you do so.

Useful verbs

The table below lists the most common and useful verbs for reporting, re-expressing and discussing source material. Note that the verbs *say*, *tell* and *mention* are not listed, as these three verbs can be a little too vague and speech-like for academic writing.

address	discuss	note
argue	dispute	point out
assert	examine	portray
challenge	exemplify	propose
claim	explain	provide
conclude	find	query
conduct	highlight	question
convey	identify	reject
define	illustrate	show
demonstrate	investigate	state
deny	justify	suggest
describe	list	trace

Key points on using these verbs

1 Choose an appropriate verb to show you understand the author's actions

Choose your verbs carefully when describing what an author is doing in their text. For example:

Mepham (2006) <u>questions</u> the method of 'learning' bioethics and <u>states</u> that a critical approach is fundamental to this field of enquiry.

Sacks et al. (2011) <u>justify</u> their recommendation to use the traffic-light system of food labelling by <u>showing</u> the …

Musssen et al. (1956) were one of the first teams to <u>trace</u> the development of a child's personality from birth to adulthood.

Each verb has a specific meaning, and if you use the wrong one your reader will think that you have not correctly understood the source text.

2 Choose an appropriate verb to show you understand the source content

In addition to using an appropriate verb for reporting what the author is doing, you need to use the correct verb for the object of that action. For example, you can't discover an experiment, measure an issue or argue a question – you conduct an experiment, measure an amount or level, and address, discuss or examine a question. For example:

Barazzone, Cavanagh and Richards (2012) <u>conducted</u> an experiment to test the effectiveness of cognitive behavioural therapy delivered online.

The 2017 World Happiness Report <u>investigates</u> and attempts to <u>measure</u> levels of happiness and well-being across different societies.

Djelic and Etchanchu (2017) <u>examine</u> whether globalisation has affected the interdependence of business and politics.

Again, if you use a verb that is not right for its object, your reader might assume that you have not understood your source material.

3 Choose an appropriate verb to show you understand the author's viewpoint

Authors often give their views in a text and also comment on the views of others, so make sure that you use a verb which reports this correctly. For example, if you want to express the fact that one author disagrees with something or someone, you will need to use verbs such as *question*, *query*, *challenge*, *dispute*, *reject* or *deny*. For example:

Carr (1968) <u>challenges</u> the assumption that when managers talk about good ethics they are expressing a true desire to behave well.

4 Choose an appropriate verb to show *your* viewpoint

You should also use verbs as a powerful tool for showing *your* attitude to a source, and/or for showing how a source supports *your* argument.

As an example, look at the sentence below from an article by Deborah Lupton:

'Research would certainly suggest that the lay public has a strong interest in health and medical issues portrayed in the media'

(Lupton 1998, p.35).

If you wanted to agree with Lupton in your essay, you might report what she says using a 'positive' verb such as *establish*, *show*, *confirm*, *demonstrate*, *identify*, *illustrate*, *inform*, *note*, *observe*, *prove* or *reveal*. For example:

Lupton (1998) <u>shows that</u> people are very interested in stories and news about medical and health matters.

You could then follow this sentence with your positive comment:

> Indeed, some of the most popular current TV shows are hospital dramas.

Note that it would be incorrect and confusing for your reader to use a positive verb to report a source and then follow this with a negative comment. Again, your reader might assume that you had not correctly understood your source material. For example:

> Lupton (1998) <u>shows</u> that people are very interested in stories and news about medical and health matters. However, I would argue that the evidence she uses to support her claim (i.e. the large amount of media coverage given to such issues) does not prove that we are interested in the medical issues per se. ✗

If you wanted to argue against Lupton and say that the public does *not* have an interest in health and medicine in the media, you would need to report Lupton in your essay using a 'neutral' verb which would then leave the way open for you to either agree or disagree with her. Commonly used neutral verbs are: *assert, assume, claim, maintain, argue, suggest* and *state*. For example, the sentence:

> Lupton (1998) <u>asserts that</u> people are very interested in stories and news about medical and health matters.

could then be followed by either:

> Indeed, some of the most popular current TV shows are hospital dramas. ✔

or

> However, I would argue the evidence she uses to support her claim (i.e. the large amount of media coverage given to such issues) does not prove that we are really interested in the medical issues per se. ✔

So you can follow a neutral verb with either a positive or a negative comment. A second example of this is given below.

> Lupton (1998) <u>maintains that</u> people are very interested in stories and news about medical and health matters. Indeed, some of the most . . . ✔

> Lupton (1998) <u>maintains that</u> people are very interested in stories and news about medical and health matters. However, I would argue that . . . ✔

5 Use the correct grammatical structure with your verb

In the active voice, all verbs need one or more of the following grammatical structures:

- Verb + that + clause. For example:
  > Lupton <u>asserts</u> <u>that</u> <u>the public is interested in medical stories</u>.
- Verb + what / why / where / who / whether + clause. For example:
  > Lockhart (2009) <u>discusses</u> <u>whether</u> <u>advertising reinforces stereotypes</u>.

- Verb + infinitive. For example:

  Keil's report <u>aims</u> <u>to cover</u> all aspects of government policy.

- Verb + noun (object). For example:

  Dawkins <u>regards</u> <u>religious education</u> as a form of indoctrination.

- Verb + -ing form (object). For example:

  Dawkins <u>regards</u> <u>teaching</u> religion as a form of indoctrination.

- Verb + object + infinitive. For example:

  The study <u>encourages</u> <u>us</u> <u>to ask</u> whether wealth distribution is desirable.

- Verb + object + preposition +-ing. For example:

  Dawkins <u>accuses</u> Gould <u>of</u> <u>pandering</u> to 'middle-of-the-road religious people' (*Times Magazine*, 2006).

Some verbs can be used with more than one grammatical structure. For example:

Lupton	<u>shows that</u>	the public is very interested in medical stories.
Lin and Moon	<u>show why</u>	the public is very interested in medical stories.
The study	<u>shows the link</u>	between folklore and history.

However, most verbs are commonly used with only one or two of the above structures.

Note that some verbs cannot be followed by *that* and must be followed by a noun/object. For example:

The novel graphically <u>portrays that</u> the horrors of the First World War. ✗

The novel graphically <u>portrays</u> the horrors of the First World War. ✔

The article essay <u>discusses that</u> the UK and American legal systems are similar. ✗

The article <u>discusses</u> the similarities between the UK and American legal system. ✔

When you are reading, try to notice which structures and words are used with verbs, and you can also use an online dictionary to help you identify the correct grammatical structure/s for particular verbs.

6 Be aware that you might need to use two or more verbs

Authors will often do more than one thing in their text, so you may often need two or more verbs. For example:

Côté and Morgan (2002) <u>conducted</u> two studies and <u>demonstrated that</u> there is a link between regulating emotions and job satisfaction.

7 Use the correct tense for reporting and discussing your sources

For advice and examples on this point, see Chapter D4, pp.153–154.

Over to You 15
Using verbs

Below are student sentences containing errors (in italics) in how the verbs used to report and discuss source material have been used. Sentences 1–9 use the wrong verb and 10 uses the correct verb but with the wrong grammatical structure. Correct the sentences. Answers and comments can be found on p.184.

1   Researchers in the UK are *undergoing studies about* the possible effects of the drug.

2   There is much evidence to *clarify* just how harmful cigarettes are.

3   Corson *imposed* that there are two main styles of English.

4   To summarise Karlov's argument, he *mentions* that playing chess uses a similar part of the brain as playing music.

5   The idea of using a computer program to collectively edit a website was *perceived* by Cunningham and Beck in the late 1990s.

6   The telephone was *established* by Alexander Bell.

7   The ideas *portrayed* in the report are not new.

8   As *implied* by Murtaz (2007), 'patient care should be the primary motive for developments in the NHS' (p. 1).

9   Laurent (2007) *claims* that 'genetic engineering is the most important advance in medicine since the development of vaccines' (p. 15). This essay will demonstrate that this is clearly the case.

10 Lupton *discusses about* the portrayal of medicine and health in the media.

C2

Discussing authors' views and position

This chapter gives you example essay sentences containing words and phrases for writing about different viewpoints and positions of source authors. (See also Chapter C3 for words to describe converging and diverging viewpoints.)

The words and phrases are underlined, with words that have similar meanings separated by /. Words that have different meanings but which can be used in similar sentence structures are separated by //. Note that where a sentence contains a reference with no year of publication it is because the year has already been given earlier in the essay from which the sentence comes.

The example sentences are followed by useful information on words that might be less familiar to you, and the chapter ends with a practice activity.

Example sentences

Points of view and positions

- This essay <u>takes / holds / subscribes to</u> <u>the view that</u> earning interest is unethical.
- Kirsch (2010) <u>thinks / holds the opinion / is of the opinion that</u> mining is not sustainable.
- Picasso <u>is</u> widely <u>regarded as / viewed as / thought of as / considered to be</u> a major influence in twentieth-century art.
- The book looks at the medieval Christian crusades <u>from the perspective / viewpoint of</u> the Muslim world.
- It is important to analyse the facts before <u>formulating a view</u>.
- <u>The view that</u> all research should help develop theory <u>is</u> debatable, <u>according to</u> May (2000).
- The article criticises the government's <u>stance / position</u> <u>on</u> potential strike action.
- Increasingly, schools are <u>positioning</u> themselves <u>within</u> a free market economy.
- I use Gordijn and Akkermans (2001) to look at e-business <u>from an</u> economic <u>perspective / viewpoint / standpoint.</u>
- Harris (2016) argues that law should be viewed <u>through the lens of / through the prism of</u> social practices.
- Increasingly, schools are <u>orientating</u> themselves <u>towards</u> a free market economy.

Views that agree, support, argue for or accept

● There <u>is</u> cross-party <u>agreement on</u> the issue of identification cards.

● Jones's 2018 study <u>supports / advocates</u> the use of the new drug.

● Patel is a <u>proponent of / advocate of / supporter of</u> civil liberties in the UK.

● The health centre <u>endorses</u> homeopathy.

● Smith is a leading <u>exponent</u> of permaculture and runs related workshops.

● <u>The argument for</u> intelligent design is that biological structures are too complex to have arisen via an undirected process.

● Diehm and Armatas (2004) look at how certain high-risk activities have been <u>accepted by</u> society.

● Penrose (2016) <u>admits / acknowledges / concedes / accepts</u> that producing a unified theory is a long-term endeavour.

● The poll showed that 61 per cent of Americans <u>condoned</u> capital punishment in cases of murder.

Views that disagree or oppose

● Svensson and Wood (2008) <u>disagree with / counter / contest / rebut / refute</u> Friedman's claim that businesses do not need to consider social issues, and state that <u>on the contrary</u>, they have a huge impact on society.

● Market socialists <u>object to the concept of</u> capitalism <u>on the grounds that</u> it leads to inequality.

● The main <u>objections</u> to the airport proposal are noise and damage to wildlife habitat.

● Dawkins (2015) <u>is opposed to / disagrees with / rejects / dismisses</u> the idea of faith schools.

● The Unionists are <u>against / averse to</u> the idea of Ireland being independent from the UK.

● <u>Opponents of</u> stem-cell research argue that there is no moral justification for using and destroying embryonic cells.

Views that are inflexible or indifferent

● The article criticises the government's <u>rigid stance / inflexible position / intransigence</u> on strike action.

● Puffer and McCarthy (1995) identified <u>ambivalence</u> about ethics in large organisations.

● Recent human rights violations indicate the government is <u>indifferent to / uninterested in</u> international opinion.

● The owner of the business should check that their board's legal advisors are <u>disinterested</u> parties.

● Many economists remain <u>sceptical</u> about the reliability of qualitative research data.

Counterarguments and alternative viewpoints

- An argument against / An argument that counters / A counterargument to the idea of evolution is that life is too complex to have developed without intelligent direction.

- A challenge to pro-capitalism ideology is that it inevitably results in the rich getting richer and the poor getting poorer.

- An alternative view / A challenge to this point of view is that capitalism is 'the greatest tool of . . . social advance ever known . . .'

Useful word information

advocate *v. n.*	*v.* To actively support.
	n. A supporter of something.
	Common phrases:
	    v. To **actively // openly // strongly advocate** X.
	    n. An **advocate of / for** X.

ambivalence *n.* **ambivalent** *adj.*	*n.* Mixed or contradictory feelings or ideas about something. Commonly confused words: *Ambivalent* and *indifferent*. These words have different meanings. See below for *indifferent*.
averse *adj.*	Opposed to. Commonly confused words: *Averse* and *adverse*. *Adverse* means unpleasant and/or harmful.
concede *v.* **concession** *n.*	*v.* To (unwillingly) admit the truth or existence of something. *n.* To make a bargain or compromise with.
condone *v.*	To accept or (reluctantly) agree with or approve of behaviour usually viewed as morally wrong. Common phrases: To condone **behaviour // the practice of // the action of // violence // abuse // torture // murder**.
counter *v.*	To respond with an opposing argument, view or action. Common phrases: To counter **a claim // an argument // a threat // a criticism**.
counterargument *n.*	A set of reasons that oppose another argument.
disinterested *adj.*	(1) Unbiased. (2) Having no interest in. Commonly confused words: *disinterested* and *uninterested*. Note that as shown by (2) above, both words can mean 'not interested', but only *disinterested* means 'unbiased and impartial'.

endorse *v.* **endorsement** *n.*	*v.* To publicly support and recommend an idea, belief, action or product.
exponent *n.*	(1) (Of people) an example, practitioner or representative of something. (2) A skilled artist or performer, usually a musician. Commonly confused words: *exponent* and *proponent* (see *proponent* below).
indifferent *adj.* **indifference** *n.*	*adj.* Having no interest in. Unconcerned. Similar to *uninterested*.
intransigent *adj.* **intransigence** *n.*	*adj.* Inflexible, unwilling to change one's mind or position.
perspective *n.*	(1) Point of view or particular understanding. (2) Representing three-dimensional space on a two-dimensional surface.
prism *n.*	In a non-literal sense, a particular way of thinking. Similar to *perspective* and *lens*. Common phrases: **Discuss / examine / analyse / see** X **through the** prism **of** Y.
proponent *n.*	Someone who puts forward or is in favour of a plan, idea or theory. Similar to *advocate* and *supporter*. *Commonly confused words: proponent and exponent.* Sometimes used interchangeably, but there is a difference in meaning. A proponent always means someone who actively and publicly supports something, whereas *exponent* has a wider range of uses and can mean someone who is an example of something but not necessarily a supporter.
sceptical *adj.* **sceptic** *n.*	*adj.* (1) Doubtful about something. (2) Questioning. In philosophy, *scepticism* is the approach whereby all knowledge and belief is questioned. The US spellings are *skeptical* and *skeptic*.
stance *n.*	A clear position on something. Common phrases: A **hard-line / tough // firm // ethical // moral** stance on X. To **adopt // hold // take** a stance **on** X.
subscribe *v.*	(1) To agree with a particular idea of way of thinking. (2) To be a member of / make regular payments to.

view *n./v.*	*n.* An opinion, belief or attitude, often not based on evidence. *v.* (1) To think of in a particular way. (2) To look at or inspect. Common phrases: A **personal // broad // narrow // simplistic // orthodox // traditional** view. To **subscribe to / hold a particular** view.
viewpoint *n.*	A particular way of thinking about something. Similar to *standpoint* and *perspective*. Commonly confused words: *viewpoint*, *view* and *point of view*. These words are often used interchangeably but strictly speaking, a *viewpoint* is a more general position from which a specific view / point of view / opinion is formed. Common phrases: A(n) **alternative // different // opposing // subjective // objective** viewpoint.

Over to You 16
Sentence correction

Below are ten sentences from student essays. The sentences are nearly but not quite right (the errors are in italics) because the student has used the wrong word or used the right word but with incorrect form or grammar. Use the examples and word information above to correct the sentences. Answers can be found on p.185.

1   There are several *disagreements* as to what constitutes an offence.

2   Brenner is a strong *advocate in* women's rights.

3   A primary *argument of* some religious groups to IVF is that it uses external fertilisation.

4   Balkin (2002) *oppose* to sex segregation in schools in that it is a diversion from more important educative issues.

5   Many pressure groups have strong *views against* embryonic research.

6   Some people *see it* as since they already pay income tax, they should not be additionally taxed on interest from savings.

7 This report has outlined the factors that *condemn against* animal testing.

8 Mueller (2011) states that people often *refute* creative ideas because they are scared of change.

9 The current government in Mexico is adopting an expansionary economic *view*.

10 A *counterclaim* to humour being used to show dominance is that it is used to relieve social tension.

C3

Comparing and connecting different authors

This chapter gives you example essay sentences containing words and phrases for comparing and connecting different sources, and for showing the relationships between them (see also Chapter C2).

The words and phrases are underlined, with words that have similar meanings separated by /. Words that have different meanings but which can be used in similar sentence structures are separated by //. Note that where a sentence contains a reference with no year of publication, it is because this has already been given earlier in the essay from which the sentence comes.

The sentences are followed by important information on words that might be less familiar to you, and the section ends with two practice activities.

Example sentences

Similar and convergent views

- <u>Both</u> Marteinson <u>and</u> Bergson view humour as arising from conflict between the real and the unreal.
- Côté and Morgan <u>are in agreement with / agree with / share the same view as / hold a similar view to</u> Hoschschild, that is, that suppressing emotions can cause stress in employees.
- Côté and Morgan, <u>together with</u> Hoschschild, <u>hold the view that</u> suppressing emotions can cause stress in workers.
- <u>Neither</u> Wolf <u>nor</u> Carr feels that businesses should concern themselves with ethics.
- Both articles <u>show / have</u> <u>considerable overlap in</u> how they view the link between literacy and reasoning.
- There <u>is</u> <u>overlap / common ground between</u> the two authors, as they both view humour as . . .
- Collins's and Esty's positions/views <u>converge</u> on the issue of business and social responsibility.

Different and divergent views

- Aristotle and others maintained that humour is used to assert superiority. <u>However,/ In contrast, / On the other hand</u>, Spencer and Freud proposed that humour serves to relieve tension.

- Aristotle and others maintained that humour is used to assert superiority. Spencer and Freud, <u>however,/ in contrast, / on the other hand</u>, proposed that humour serves to relieve tension.

- <u>Whereas / Although</u> Wolf believes that business operates separately from society, Svensson and Wood show that the two are mutually dependent.

- Wolf <u>suggests that</u> business should operate separately from society, <u>while / whereas</u> Svensson and Wood show that they are interdependent.

- Wolf <u>states that</u> business and society should act separately from each other, but <u>opponents of this view</u> suggest that the two are co-dependent.

- There are <u>diverse / varied / different</u> opinions as to whether ethics have a valid place in a business.

- The literature reveals two <u>different / distinct / discrete</u> theories.

- <u>Although both</u> Miller and Hurley <u>agree</u> that humour is connected to sexual selection, <u>they disagree on / their views differ in regard to / they diverge on</u> the extent of the role humour plays.

- Miller's <u>view differs from that of</u> Hurley's <u>as to</u> the degree of importance humour has in evolutionary selection.

Describing how one source cites another as support and/or comments positively

- Barrick et al. (2002) <u>cite</u> Bakan as a proponent of the idea that achieving status is a key goal in social interaction.

- Halle <u>quotes</u> from Le Corbusier (1986) <u>as support for his argument that</u> abstract art has been idealised in art theory.

- Hepner <u>paraphrases / uses paraphrases from //</u> <u>quotes from / uses quotations from</u> the Bible <u>as justification for</u> his ideas.

- Hepner uses Bible <u>extracts / excerpts</u> <u>(in an attempt) to defend / justify</u> his ideas.

- <u>According to</u> Woolf, Austen <u>made a great contribution to</u> fiction, despite not having a private writing space.

- Woolf <u>acknowledged</u> Austen's contribution to fiction and the fact that she wrote despite not having any private space.

- Jung <u>credited</u> Gross <u>with</u> hav<u>ing</u> preceded him in identifying two distinct types of consciousness.

Describing how sources respond to, challenge and criticise each other

- <u>According to</u> Phillipson (2000), Crystal has a Eurocentric view of English as a global language.

- Crystal (2000) <u>responds to / replies to</u> Phillipson's criticism <u>by stating that</u> he merely describes how English is used.

- Svensson and Wood (2008) <u>disagree with / contest / refute</u> Friedman's claim that businesses do not need to consider social issues and state that <u>on the contrary,</u> businesses have an enormous impact on society.

- Ainsworth <u>counters / rebuts</u> Dawkins's claim that faith schools are discriminatory <u>by proposing / with the proposition / by maintaining / by asserting</u> that such schools allow children informed choice.

- Guthrie and Parker (1989) offer <u>a rebuttal of</u> Legitimacy Theory. They suggest that . . .

- Lupton (1998) <u>challenges / questions</u> Fox's suggestion that doctors are no longer seen as the authorities on medical issues.

- Gould <u>is (strongly / vigorously) challenged by</u> Dawkins, who accuses him of writing for 'middle-of- the-road religious people'.

- Phillipson has <u>criticised</u> linguists such as Crystal for having a Eurocentric view of the global dominance of English.

- Smith's main <u>criticism of</u> Dawkins's position is that he overstates the role religion plays in human conflict.

- Watson and Crick <u>failed to credit</u> Franklin in their initial publication on the structure of DNA.

Useful word information

according to *adv.*	(1) As stated by. (2) Corresponding to or in proportion to. E.g. Business should trade according to government regulations. NB. *According to* is only used to refer to others, not oneself.
acknowledge *v.*	(1) To accept, admit or show gratitude for something. (2) In academic writing, to reference / cite an author.
assert *v.* **assertion** *n.*	*v.* (1) To state a fact or belief. (2) To force others to recognise one's authority. *n.* A statement of fact or belief.
cite *v.* **citation** *n.*	*v.* To refer to someone or something else, usually as evidence or support. NB. Use *cite* only to describe when one author mentions another. It is incorrect to say 'I cite '. Commonly confused words: *cite*, *site* and *sight*. Note the different spellings of these three different words.
contest *v./n.*	*v.* To argue against a statement and to attempt to prove it is false. Similar to *rebut* but more commonly used. Common phrases: To contest the **claim // suggestion // accusation // idea // theory** that ...

converge *v.* **convergence** *n.* **convergent** *adj.*	*v.* Of directions or viewpoints, to come or start to come together.
counter *v./adj./adv.*	*v.* To respond with an opposing argument, view or action. NB. The phrase 'X **is counter to** Y' / 'X **runs counter to** Y' is when an action (accidentally or purposely) goes against something else. Common phrases: To counter **a claim // an argument // a threat // a criticism**.
diverge *v.* **divergence** *n.* **divergent** *adj.*	*v.* To go or to start to go in different directions.
excerpt *n.*	*n.* A short section from a book, film or piece of music. Similar to *extract.*
extract *n./v.*	*n* . (1) A short section from a book, film or piece of music. Similar to *excerpt.* (2) A concentrated food or chemical preparation.
maintain *v.*	*Maintain* has several different meanings. In the context of evaluating sources, it means to state something clearly and confidently (with or without evidence) often in the face of criticism. Similar to *assert* and *claim.*
paraphrase *v./n.*	To express the meaning of writing or speech using different words, often in order to clarify or simplify.
quote *v./n.*	*v.* To use the exact words of someone else. NB *Quote* is used to describe when one source quotes another. It is incorrect to say 'I quote . . .' or 'Smith quotes that . . .' Commonly confused words: *quote / quotation* and *cite / citation.* *Citation* is sometimes used to mean *quotation.* However, a citation is a broader term that can refer to any type of reference to a source, including just the author's name.
rebut *v.* **rebuttal** *n.*	*v.* To argue against a statement. Similar to *contest* but less commonly used.
refute *v.*	To oppose and prove that the statement is false. Common phrases: To refute the **claim // suggestion // accusation // idea // theory** that … .

reject *v./n.*	*v.* To not accept. Commonly confused words: *reject*, *refute* and *deny*. *Reject* has the more general meaning. *Refute* is more formal and differs from both *reject* and *deny* because it includes giving reasons for not accepting a statement. *To deny* often means to reject an accusation and is not usually appropriate in an academic context.

Over to You 17
Sentence correction

Below are ten sentences from student essays. The sentences are nearly but not quite right because the student has used the wrong word or used the right word but with incorrect form or grammar (errors are in italics). Use the examples and word information above to correct the sentences. Answers can be found on p.186.

1   *According to me*, the issue of global warming is not as serious as the media portrays.

2   Kerlinger (1969) *quotes* that 'Science is a misused and misunderstood word' (p.1127).

3   It has been *alleged* that computer games can be used to educate children.

4   Smith (2009) has criticised Ramone's work *as* being overcomplicated.

5   Karl Marx *refuted* capitalism as a positive system for social development.

6   According to Gilchrist, *he suggests that* we need to re-evaluate how we perceive risk-taking heroines, particularly those who are also mothers.

7   Kroll *states* Frie as an example of how early approaches to second-language learning saw teaching writing as secondary to speech.

8   The research team *knowledge* that their data is incomplete and that further studies are needed.

9   According to (*Dr Reynolds, 2000*) there is no strong evidence of long-term damage to health.

10 As Collins (1994) *cites*, 'good ethics is synonymous with good management.' (p.2).

Over to You 18
Synthesising sources

Below are brief summaries of three different theories of job satisfaction. Write a paragraph that compares and connects these three sources using vocabulary from this section. An example paragraph is given on p.186.

Summaries

1. Locke 's theory states that what a person wants to do in a job (their 'conscious goals and intentions') and how far these goals are achieved, are the main factors that determine job satisfaction (Locke, 1968).

2. The dispositional approach sees a person's disposition as the most important element in determining their level of job satisfaction, regardless of the job type (Staw, Bell and Clausen, 1986).

3. The most complex model proposes that organisational structure influences the characteristics of a job, and that jobs with particular characteristics attract people with particular personality attributes. These attributes determine how satisfied a person will be with their job (Oldham and Hackman, 1981) and therefore both job type and employee personality are central to determining job satisfaction.

References

Locke, E. A. (1968) 'Towards a Theory of Task Motivation and Incentives', Organisational Behaviour and Human Performance *3(2), pp.157–189.*

Oldham, G. and Hackman, J. (1981) 'Relationships Between Organisational Structure and Employee Reactions: Comparing Alternative Frameworks', Administrative Science Quarterly *26(1), pp.66–83.*

Staw, B., Bell, N. and Clausen, J. (1986) 'The Dispositional Approach To Job Attributes: A Lifetime Longitudinal Test', Administrative Science Quarterly *31(1), pp.56–77.*

C4

Making positive comments

This chapter gives you example essay sentences containing words and phrases for evaluating a source positively, and for showing how the author's views support your own argument.

The words and phrases are underlined, with words that have similar meanings separated by /. Words that have different meanings but which can be used in similar sentence structures are separated by //. Note that where a sentence contains a reference but no year of publication, it is because this has already been given earlier in the essay from which the sentence comes.

The sentences are followed by important information on words that might be less familiar to you, and the section ends with a practice activity.

Example sentences

Using neutral verbs to introduce a source and then give a positive comment

- Aknin et al. (2018) assert / claim / contend / maintain / propose / suggest / state that throughout our development, positive emotional states encourage us to behave more positively to others. Other studies support this idea . . .

- Vellitino examines // considers / takes into account // covers in detail the four different concepts of dyslexia. He shows that . . .

Using positive verbs to comment on a source

- The authors demonstrate / illustrate / show / establish that well-run businesses are of benefit to society. Their findings . . .

- Skinner found that reinforcement strengthens patterns of behaviour.

- Stich (1985) provides illuminating examples human irrationality. The most interesting is . . .

- Milanovic (2002) explains // demonstrates / illustrates / shows how globalisation can affect income distribution.

- Martin and Thompson (2010) examine // cover in detail // consider / take into account the different definitions and types of social enterprises.

- Keegan and Bosilie (2006) found that // observed that / made the observation that / noted that // established that HRM journals tend to exclude articles that are highly critical of HR practices.

- The author's argument is <u>validated by / supported by / justified by</u> the data presented in my report.
- Perdue and Gurtman (1990) <u>identify</u> a previously overlooked factor in ageism, namely . . .
- Miller (1991) <u>explicates</u> the process by which people developmental models of relationships. He illustrates how . . .
- Rubia investigates aspects of neuropsychology and <u>clarifies</u> the nature of psychiatric disorders.
- The article successfully <u>simplifies</u> the complex theory of special relativity.
- The report <u>benefits from</u> rigorous research, a succinct style and a readable format.

Using positive adjectives, adverbs and nouns to comment on a source

- Helliwell et al. (2018) give a <u>comprehensive / thorough // extensive</u> overview of levels of social happiness across the globe and offer <u>clear // useful insights</u> into . . .
- Bergl and Vigilant (2007) provide <u>important // interesting // reliable / sound</u> data on Cross River gorilla migration. Their data . . .
- Perez et al. (2017) provide <u>overwhelming // compelling // convincing // objective / hard // strong // clear // ample</u> evidence that . . .
- Their research <u>conclusively // convincingly</u> shows / establishes that active transport policies in a city can have many health and economic benefits.
- In my view, Perdue and Gurtman (1990) <u>correctly</u> identify an important and previously overlooked factor in ageism, namely . . .
- He provides a <u>coherent // cogent / logical / sound / valid / reasonable / considered</u> argument to support his theory that . . .
- Skinner puts forward <u>innovative // convincing / persuasive / plausible / credible</u> ideas about teaching methodology.
- Stich (1985) provides <u>illuminating examples</u> of human irrationality. The most interesting is . . .
- The report benefits from <u>rigorous</u> research, a <u>succinct</u> style and a <u>readable</u> format.
- <u>A clear strength of</u> the survey is the very large sample size.

Stating that source is supported by other research or has contributed to the field

- The idea proposed by Valencia-Flores et al. (2002) that the 'siesta culture' of Mexican students is a negative stereotype is <u>supported / corroborated / confirmed / verified / validated / substantiated by</u> other research in this area. Studies by . . .
- Importantly, the findings are <u>consistent with</u> those of previous studies.
- His <u>substantive</u> body of work has <u>influenced</u> many areas of psychology. The most important area has been . . .

● Djelic and Etchanchu's 2017 article is a <u>noteworthy // valuable // substantive</u> <u>contribution to</u> the debate on corporate responsibility because . . .

Useful word information

assert *v.* **assertion** *n.*	*v.* (1) To state a fact or belief. (2) To force others to recognise one's authority. *n.* A statement of fact or belief. An assertion can include statements that are not argued or tested.
claim *v./n.*	To state something clearly and confidently, with or without evidence. Similar to *maintain*. Common phrases: To **make a / the** claim.
cogent *adj.*	Logical, clear and convincing. Usually used in the context of an argument. Common phrases: A cogent **argument // case**. To **put forward / propose** a cogent **argument // case**.
coherent *adj.*	Logical, well-structured and consistent. Common phrases: A coherent **argument // article // framework // strategy // policy // system // theory**. To do X **in a** coherent **way / manner.** Commonly confused words: *coherent*, *cogent* and *cohesive*. *Coherent* and *cogent* are often used interchangeably, but strictly speaking a coherent argument is well-structured but not necessarily cogent (convincing). *Cohesive* means 'sticking together' and is used in the context of physical things and groups rather than to describe argument, e.g. 'They are a cohesive team.'
compelling *adj.*	Convincing.
comprehensive *adj.*	Covering all or nearly all aspects, wide-ranging. Similar to *thorough*. Common phrases: (A) comprehensive **review // examination // study // account // coverage // survey**.
conclusive *adj.* **conclusively** *adv.*	*adj.* Of an argument or evidence, strong and convincing. Common phrases: X **is / provides / gives // shows** conclusive **proof / evidence // results**.

consistent *adj.*	(1) Does not contradict. (2) Unchanging. Common phrases: A consistent **approach // standard // level**. X is consistent with the **aim // data // evidence / findings // objective //principle // view of** Y.
contend *v.* **contention** *n.*	*v.* To state something to be argued, with or without evidence. Similar to *argue*. *n.* A declaration of fact or belief to be argued. Similar to *assertion*.
corroborate *v.*	*v.* To confirm or give support to something else. Used in the context of statements and data rather than ideas.
credible *adj.*	Authoritative and convincing. Common phrases: (A) credible **source // evidence // data // argument // explanation // threat // deterrent**. **Scientifically // politically // academically** credible.
explicate *v.* **explication** *n.*	To analyse and develop an idea, theory or argument. Commonly confused words: *explicate* and *explain*. *To explicate* means to analyse (break down and explore) something at a deep level. For example: 'The third paragraph of this explication looks at how the poem's rhythm adds to its meaning.' *To explain* means to give a description of something and/ or to give the reasons why something happens or exists. For example: 'The appendix gives an explanation of the different categories of hospital.'
extensive *adj.*	(1) Covering many aspects of an issue or idea, e.g. an extensive survey. (2) Covering a wide area. Commonly confused words*: extensive, comprehensive* and *exhaustive*. There is overlap but also some difference in meaning. *Extensive* = covering many aspects. *Comprehensive* = covering all or nearly all aspects. *Exhaustive* = covering absolutely all aspects.
illuminate *v.* **illuminating** *adj.*	*adj.* (1) Providing clarity and understanding. Similar to *insightful*. (2) Providing light. Common phrases: An illuminating **example // discussion // piece of research // experience**.

illustrate *v.* **illustration** *n.*	(1) To give an example and/or to demonstrate. (2) To use / provide with pictures. Common phrases: To illustrate **a point // argument // principle //** **concept**. To illustrate the / a **importance // complexity //** **difficulty // problem // concept // model**. X **seeks to / attempts to / tries to // serves to** illustrate Y.
maintain *v.*	*Maintain* has several different meanings. In the context of evaluating sources *maintain* means to state something clearly and confidently (with or without evidence) often in the face of criticism. Similar to *claim.*
noteworthy *adj.*	Worth special attention.
plausible *adj.*	Seeming to be reasonable and believable. Common phrases: A plausible **explanation // theory // argument //** **hypothesis // idea // interpretation**.
substantiate *v.*	To provide supporting evidence or information. Similar to *corroborate* and *support.*
substantive *adj.*	(1) Dealing with real-world issues and facts, and having importance and impact. (2) Important, main. Commonly confused words: *Substantive* and *substantial.* *Substantial* means of a large size or quantity. Common phrases: A substantive **issue // body of work // report //** **piece of research**.
succinct *adj.*	Brief and clear.
valid *adj.* **validity** *n.* **validate** *v.*	*adj.* (1) Legal. (2) Logically justified or supported by evidence. *v.* To confirm or prove. Common phrases: **Scientifically // statistically // logically** valid. A valid **argument // assumption // opinion //** **belief // viewpoint // interpretation //** **explanation**.
verify *v.*	To check or show something to be true.

Over to You 19
Sentence correction

Below are ten sentences from student essays. The sentences are nearly but not quite right, because the student has used the wrong word, or used the right word but with incorrect form or grammar (errors are in italics). Use the examples and word information above to correct the sentences. Answers can be found on p.187.

1   The new company is extremely *innovated*.

2   The National Bureau of Economic Research has been *a great benefit for* the field of economics in recent years.

3   I will look at both the theoretical and *substantial* implications of recent research on the consequences of job insecurity.

4   Lupton (1998) *shows* that the public is interested in health news. However, I will argue that media coverage in this area does not necessarily indicate genuine public interest.

5   Oswald's research *corroborates* the idea that having a job is more significant for happiness than being wealthy.

6   Jack, James and Roger's explanation of the effect of caffeine on performance seems to me the most *possible* because . . .

7   The *viability* of this belief is called into question by recent evidence.

8   Although the survey is *comprehensive*, it fails to look at applications of learning curve theory.

9   Carr (1968) uses the *illustrating* analogy of a poker player to demonstrate his position on business ethics.

10 Importantly, the findings are *consistent to* those of previous studies.

C5

Making negative comments

This chapter gives you example essay sentences containing words and phrases for introducing, describing and evaluating a source negatively. An important part of developing your argument is to present opposing arguments, and to show why they are not as convincing as your own.

The words and phrases are underlined, with words that have similar meanings separated by /. Words that have different meanings but that can be used in similar sentence structures are separated by //. Note that where a sentence contains a reference but no year of publication, it is because this has already been given earlier in the essay from which the sentence comes.

The sentences are followed by important information on words which might be less familiar to you, and the section ends with two practice activities.

Example sentences

Using *not* with positive verbs to give a negative comment

- Jones (2016) <u>does not show / demonstrate / establish</u> that the virus has mutated.
- Tran (2018) <u>does not consider / take into account</u> companies in which Asian and Western approaches to SR have merged.

Using neutral verbs to introduce a source and then give a negative comment

- In 1984, Levitt <u>stated // suggested // asserted / contended / claimed / maintained / proposed</u> that the world was becoming a 'global village'. My proposition is that this term is <u>not</u> useful because . . .
- The report <u>proposes // states // suggests</u> that all students should do an internship. This is <u>not</u> a sensible policy because . . .
- Shaw (2016) <u>tends to</u> overcomplicate some aspects of business ethics. For example, he . . .

Using negative verbs to comment on a source

- Keegan and Bosilie (2006) <u>neglect / overlook / omit // ignore</u> the fact that critical views about business models might be contained within articles whose titles purport to be uncritical.

- The authors <u>fail to</u> draw a distinction between how adults and children behave in the situation.

- The study <u>complicates</u> what is in fact a relatively simple concept.

- The report <u>suffers from</u> a lack of detailed analysis.

- Miller's (1991) model of relationships has been <u>disproved / discredited // superseded</u> by . . . . The fact that there are several digressions <u>detracts</u> from the main argument.

- The diagrams and tables <u>distract</u> the reader from the main point of the text.

- The study <u>manipulates / distorts</u> the findings to fit in with the author's initial proposition.

- In my view, we can <u>disregard / discount</u> the idea that personality has a major effect on second language acquisition because . . .

- The small sample size should <u>alert</u> us to the fact that the findings may be unreliable.

- Alwald's conclusion <u>conflicts with / contradicts</u> his earlier point that we need new legislation on drug use.

- I suggest that the concept of 'social happiness' is <u>misconceived</u> because . . .

- Batiste's view that discoveries are made by developing and then testing a theory, <u>oversimplifies</u> the process.

Using adjectives and adverbs to comment negatively on a source

- Smith's argument is <u>invalid / flawed / unsound // inconsistent // incoherent // contradictory // problematic // circular // unconvincing</u> because . . .

- Smith's study is <u>inconclusive // limited // questionable // unreliable // unsatisfactory</u> because . . .

- Alwald's evidence seems <u>subjective // anecdotal // contradictory // incomplete</u>. He fails to . . .

- The questions used in the survey seem somewhat <u>arbitrary // simplistic // obscure // opaque.</u>

- The report's conclusion is <u>vague</u>. It does not specify . . .

- Ariti et al.'s (2018) study has <u>limited application</u> because it only looks at one specific region in Ethiopia.

- The company's so-called innovative and coherent strategy is in fact <u>formulaic // derivative // discursive</u>.

- I will show that Peccori <u>wrongly</u> assumes that the correlation between work stress and drug use is a causal one.

Using nouns to comment negatively on a source

- There are practical <u>objections to / problems with</u> Noah and Gee's idea of rewarding compliance.

- A <u>weakness in / limitation of</u> the argument is that it does not distinguish between men and women.
- A (common) <u>criticism</u> of this study is that any measurement of happiness is largely subjective.
- <u>The problem with</u> Kohil's argument is that it does not cover all possible situations.
- One <u>flaw</u> in the study is that it is <u>biased</u> towards Western cultures.
- The argument that business and society are separate is, as I will demonstrate, a <u>fallacy</u>.
- The research team seem to show <u>a disregard for</u> proper contamination control.
- Tse <u>offers no explanation</u> as to how employees might benefit from rationalisation.
- The report suffers from <u>a lack of / absence of</u> detailed analysis.
- A <u>conspicuous / noticeable</u> <u>omission</u> is that the report's analysis does not include children.
- There are several <u>digressions</u>, and the many anecdotes are <u>a distraction</u> from the main point of the paper.
- The authors make <u>no attempt to</u> present or evaluate the counterarguments.

Identifying flaws in the logic of an argument

- The absence of women in the study means that his conclusions are an <u>overgeneralisation</u>.
- Saying that an opt-out system is good because it ensures organs are donated unless specified otherwise is a <u>circular</u> argument.
- Arguing that because identity theft is increasing we should introduce identity cards is a <u>non sequitur.</u>
- Ormazabal (2003) argues that there is a <u>contradiction</u> in Keynes's definition of income.
- The report uses the <u>tautological statement / tautology</u> that the economy will either improve or will not.
- The report offers the <u>truism</u> that to achieve good public health we need adequate health funding.
- The argument that economic growth always increases social happiness is <u>irrational / illogical</u> because . . .

Stating that an argument is not supported by other research

- Lock's idea is <u>not corroborated by / not supported by // contradictory to // undermined by</u> other research.
- This claim is <u>called into question by / conflicts with / is contradicted by / is inconsistent with</u> later studies.

Stating how research or an argument could have been better

- The report <u>would have been more convincing // persuasive // effective if it had</u> used more recent data.

Conceding up to a point but then disagreeing

- Translators <u>are necessary but</u> can't always convey fully the author's meaning.
- <u>Although necessary, I have shown that</u> translators can't always convey the author's exact meaning.
- <u>Notwithstanding the fact that / Despite the fact that</u> translators are essential, they often can't convey . . .
- Translators are essential. <u>Nonetheless, / Nevertheless, / However,</u> I have shown that they cannot . . .
- <u>While I don't agree with</u> Dawkins that religious education is indoctrination, <u>I do think that</u> he <u>has a valid point when</u> he says . . .
- <u>Although I think it is going too far to say that</u> unions are redundant, <u>we should be willing to concede / accept / acknowledge that</u> . . .
- <u>I disagree with</u> Collins <u>on the extent to which</u> businesses should be ethical, <u>but I do agree with</u> his basic proposition.

Stating clearly that you disagree

- I <u>do not agree with / disagree with // refute / contest // reject // rebut</u> Lei's claim and offer the alternative suggestion that . . .

Suggesting counterarguments

- <u>An argument against / An argument that counters / A counterargument to</u> the proposition that we do not need continued economic growth is that humans have an inbuilt need to innovate and grow.
- <u>A challenge to</u> capitalism <u>is that</u> it results in the rich getting richer and the poor getting poorer.
- There is evidence for man-made causes of global warming but <u>an alternative</u> theory <u>is that</u> . . .
- I <u>counter</u> Wolf's hypothesis <u>with the suggestion that</u> businesses and society are interdependent.
- My <u>rebuttal</u> of the argument that B personalities are better than Type A is based on the fact that . . .
- The main problem with Bernhard's hypothesis is that it is too restrictive. <u>I therefore / thus offer an / the alternative suggestion / view, which is that</u> . . .
- I would <u>argue that the opposite is probably / likely to be the case</u> because . . .

Useful word information

anecdotal *adj.*	Coming from casual observation rather than objective data. NB. The noun *anecdote* means 'a short entertaining story'.
arbitrary *adj.*	Actions or decisions based on unjustified, random premises and assumptions.
bias *n.*	Unequal or unfair treatment.
circular *adj.*	A logical fallacy whereby an argument is 'empty' because the conclusion is merely a restatement of the premise(s) and so assumes as true what it is trying to prove.
conspicuous *adj.*	Clearly visible, noticeable. Often (but not always) used in a negative context. Common phrases: A conspicuous **flaw // deficiency // absence**.
contest *n./v.*	*v.* To argue against something. Similar to *refute* and *rebut*. Common phrases: To contest the **claim // idea // theory // suggestions // accusation** that . . .
contradiction *n.* **contradict** *v.* **contradictory** *adj.*	*n.* In argument, such that two or more statements cannot both/all be true.
counter *v./adj./adv.*	*v.* To respond with an opposing argument, view or action. Common phrases: To counter **a claim // an argument // a threat // a criticism.** NB The phrase 'X **is counter to** Y' / 'X **runs counter to** Y' is when an action (accidentally or purposely) goes against something else.
counterargument *n.*	An argument that opposes another one. Commonly confused words: *Counterargument* and *counterclaim*. In academic study you can counter a claim someone makes. However, the noun and verb where these two words are put together – *counterclaim* – are usually only used in legal and insurance contexts.

detract *v.* **detraction** *n.*	*v.* To reduce the value or worth of something or to make it seem less impressive. Commonly confused words: *detract* and *distract* (see below).
digress *v.* **digression** *n.*	*v.* To move away from the main topic / issue.
discount *v./n.*	*v.* (1) To disregard or leave out something because it lacks validity and/or importance. (2) To deduct from the original price.
discredit *v.*	(1) In academic study, to cause evidence or ideas to seem unreliable or false. (2) To damage someone's reputation in some way. Common phrases: To discredit an **argument // idea // theory // research**.
distort *v.* **distortion** *n.*	*v.* To give a misleading or false impression, or to misrepresent. Common phrases: To distort (the) **facts // evidence // findings // results // truth // understanding // reality**.
distract *v.* **distraction** *n.*	*v.* To take away attention, concentration or focus from something else. Common phrases: X distracts Y from the **main aim / goal / purpose / objective**. Commonly confused words: *distract* and *detract*. See above for *detract*.
fallacy *n.* **fallacious** *adj.*	*n.* (1) A commonly held but false idea or belief. (2) In formal logic, any form of incorrect reasoning that causes an invalid argument. Examples of logical fallacies are *non sequitur* (see below) and *false analogy*.
flaw *n.* **flawed** *adj.*	*n.* A defect, shortcoming or underlying weakness.
formulaic *adj.*	Not original or interesting because it uses a standard and much-used format.
incoherent *adj.*	Not logical and poorly structured.
inconclusive *adj.*	Not producing a definite result or conclusion. Common phrases: To **be // remain // prove** inconclusive.

inconsistent *adj.*	(1) Unstable, changing in some way, or acting in a different way than previously. (2) Contradictory.
invalid *adj.* **invalidity** *n.*	*adj.* (1) In logic, an invalid argument is one that contains flawed reasoning, i.e. where the conclusion does not necessarily follow from the premises. A non sequitur is an example of an invalid argument (see below). (2) Not legally recognised.
manipulate *v.*	(1) To alter or present information in a way that is purposely misleading. (2) To move, handle or control, usually by using the hands. (3) To influence and/or control another person.
misconceive *v.* **misconception** *n.*	*v.* (1) To plan or judge something poorly or incorrectly. (2) To misunderstand. *n.* An incorrect belief or opinion.
non sequitur *n.*	A statement that does not follow logically from the one before, or when a conclusion is based on insufficient, incorrect or irrelevant reasoning. In formal logic, a non sequitur is when a conclusion does not follow from its premise(s). For example: This bike has a puncture, so I won't wear a coat.
objection *n.* **object** *v./n.*	*n.* A reason for disagreeing with or disapproving of something. Common phrases: A **chief / main /primary /principal // fundamental // formal** objection.
omission *n.* **omit** *v.*	*n.* Something left out, or a failure to do something.
overgeneralise *v.* **overgeneralisation** *n.*	*v.* To apply a specific case to a wider range of situations (to generalise) that is too broad to be justified, e.g. 'People are healthier now than they were twenty years ago.'
oversimplify *v,* **oversimplification** *n.*	*v.* To explain something (usually a cause and effect process) so that it seems simpler than it actually is, e.g. 'Sugar makes you fat.' Commonly confused words: *overgeneralise* and *oversimplify*. As shown in the definitions here, an overgeneralisation is a statement that is incorrect because it is applied too broadly, not because it oversimplifies a situation or process.
questionable *adj.*	(1) Open to doubt or challenge regarding quality, accuracy or truth. (2) Of someone's character, not very honest or respectable.

rebut *v.* **rebuttal** *n.*	*v.* To argue against a statement and attempt to show that it is false. Similar to *contest* and *refute* but less commonly used.
refute *n.*	To oppose a statement and try to prove that the statement is false. Similar to *contest* and *rebut*. Common phrases: To refute the **claim // suggestion // accusation // idea // theory** that . . .
reject *v./n.*	To not accept. Commonly confused words: *reject*, *refute* and *deny*. *Reject* has the more general meaning. *To refute* is a more formal word used only in the context of argument and ideas. If you refute something you must include your reasons for not accepting the statement. *To deny* often means to reject an accusation or the truth of something, and is not usually appropriate in an academic context.
simplistic *adj.*	(Much) simpler than is actually the case, and therefore misleading. Common phrases: A simplistic **approach // argument // assumption // description // explanation // view**.
subjective *adj.*	Based on feelings and beliefs rather than evidence or fact. Opposite of *objective*.
tautology *n.* **tautological** *adj.*	*n.* A sentence or phrase that merely repeats itself. Tautologies are common in everyday language. For example: 'A free gift', 'joined together', 'in close proximity'.
truism *n.*	An obviously true and uninteresting statement that is therefore not worth making. Commonly confused words: *truism* and *axiom*. These words can be interchanged, but an axiom can also refer to a statement that is useful because it establishes a basic premise or principle from which to analyse an argument. *Axiom* in this positive sense is often used in mathematics and philosophy. The adjective *axiomatic* (in the sense of obviously true/ uninteresting) is quite common in academic writing, e.g. 'It's axiomatic to say that economic growth relies on production.'

undermine *v.*	To cause something to become less confident, successful or powerful. Common phrases: To undermine **credibility** // **validity** // **trust** // **support** // **confidence** // **value** // **stability** // **democracy**. To undermine a/an **principle** // **argument** // **belief** // **idea** // **theory**.
vague *adj.*	Imprecise, indefinite or unclear. Commonly confused words: *vague* and *ambiguous.* These words have different meanings. Something is ambiguous if it has more than one possible meaning and so may be interpreted differently in different contexts.

Over to You 20
Sentence correction

Below are ten sentences from student essays. The sentences are nearly but not quite right because the student has used the wrong word, or used the right word but with incorrect form or grammar (errors are in italics). Use the examples and word information above to correct the sentences. Answers can be found on p.187.

1   To state that cancer is caused by obesity is an *overgeneralisation*.

2   The study *alleged* that mass media can be used to educate children but this was not borne out by the evidence.

3   The conclusion is contradicted *with* the data given earlier in the paper.

4   Tanen (2000) *established* that visual imprinting occurs in infancy. However, this was shown to be incorrect by later studies.

5   Bijal (2002) *fails to neglect* the fact that in most urban areas rich and poor sometimes live in close proximity.

6   Smith's study is *limiting* because the sample size is extremely small.

7   The experiment was conducted according to a *formulaic* method in order to ensure reliability.

8   The arguments in Bazer's article have a strong *bias* of Eurocentric.

9   Hooper's theory of the origin of the HIV virus is *suffering from* lack of evidence.

10   The theory was *given discredit* in 2001, when it was shown that there was no evidence to support it.

Over to You 21
Evaluating a source negatively

Below is part of the student's critical analysis of the Albert Carr article from pp.32–33. Use this informal analysis to write a more formal essay paragraph that comments negatively on the article.

   An example essay paragraph can be found on p.188.

Extract from the student's informal critical analysis of the Carr article

His style is quite persuasive – I instinctively feel he is partly right – but he is very cynical and oversimplifies. He gives no evidence for his views and doesn't try to be objective or look at opposing evidence. His argument isn't very well-ordered as it is continuous opinion rather than a developed argument. I agree with Carr that some people feel they do need to lie in business but not that this is always the case or that business ethics are totally separate from social norms – not true nowadays?

Part D

Checking and correcting your work

Being clear and precise

To write successfully you need to be able to communicate complex ideas precisely; vague or incorrect language will lessen the clarity and credibility of your work. In Part C we looked at useful vocabulary to use when you integrate, describe and discuss your reading in your essays. Part D of this book looks at useful language points that will help you write in a formal style that is also clear, precise and to the point.

Students are often concerned about how formal their writing needs to be. The appropriate level of formality will vary slightly according to your discipline, writing aims and reader audience, but in general, producing good academic writing does *not* mean using as many long words as possible. If a book or academic article you read is written in a style so complex and wordy that it is difficult to make sense of, it is probably poorly written. Your academic writing should be clear and succinct, and you should never use a word you don't understand. Your tutors would much rather have you explain things well in clear, simple words and sentences than try to explain things poorly in more complex language.

Use nouns

Good academic writing makes it easy for the reader to identify the key ideas, and a successful piece of writing also often needs to convey complex and abstract ideas in a relatively short space of text. The main way of achieving these two things is to express ideas, information and concepts as nouns and noun phrases, and to use a structure that puts them at or near the start of the sentence.

Below is an example of this technique. Sentence A uses mainly subject/verb phrases (in bold) while sentence B has more noun phrases (in bold). Sentence B is a more effective piece of academic writing because it gives the reader the key idea quickly and clearly.

A 'Many **people** in the survey **said** that the thing that **made them** most **happy** at work was whether **they felt they were doing** a good job or not.'

B '**The data** show that **job satisfaction** is the most important **factor** in **happiness** at work.'

One word of caution with using nouns – although using them is a good thing, too many abstract nouns (words that end in *-tion, -ism, -ness, -nce, -ity*) in one sentence can sound clumsy and be unclear. In these cases it is better to use a mix of nouns and the subject/verb forms instead. For example:

The **organisation** of the **compilation** of the **legislation** was poor. ✗

The **compilation** of the legislation **was poorly organised.** ✓

Over to You 22
Using nouns

Read the two paraphrases below and then the commentary. Both paraphrases give the same correct information (the results of a study conducted by Côté and Morgan in 2008) but in two different writing styles.

Paraphrase 1

Côté and Morgan did an experiment, and they showed that people make or pretend to make themselves feel happier more often than they try to hide feeling unhappy or angry. Another important thing they found out was that the way you hide or alter your feelings can have a big effect on how happy you are with your job and whether or not you think you want to leave it. However, they didn't find any evidence that people are affected the other way round, that how you feel about your job and leaving it affects how much you hide or change your emotions.

Paraphrase 2

Côté and Morgan's data showed that the amplification of pleasant emotions happened more frequently than the suppression of unpleasant ones. Importantly, they also found a strong correlation between emotion regulation and job satisfaction and intention to quit. However, there was no strong evidence to suggest the reverse correlation, namely, that job satisfaction and intention to quit influence emotional regulation.

Comments

Paraphrase 1 is written in a fairly informal style, with lots of subject and verb phrases (e.g. *people make, they try to hide, the way you hide, if you think, how you feel*). You may quite like this style, and there is nothing grammatically incorrect about it; however, the constant use of *they/you* is too personal for academic writing, and also distracts the reader from the information being discussed.

Paraphrase 2 is written in a more formal style that tends to use nouns (*amplification, emotions, suppression, correlation, job satisfaction, intention, emotional regulation*) rather than subject/verb phrases. This gives more emphasis to the information and makes the extract more clear, concise and powerful.

Avoid sentences that are too long or too short

A sentence that has four or more clauses might be grammatically correct but will be difficult for your reader to follow. For example, the following sentence is too long:

> This essay has explained two common issues Chinese teenagers have in learning English, firstly physiological problems, including the strong emotions that adolescence brings to many teenagers and the stress of college entrance exams, and secondly the fact that the education system is highly exam-oriented, which encourages teachers to make their classes very grammar-focused and so perceived by the students as not very relevant to real life.

It would be clearer for the reader if the above sentence were split into three separate ones:

> This essay has explained two common issues Chinese teenagers have in learning English. The first is physiological problems, including the strong emotions that adolescence brings to many teenagers and the stress of college entrance exams. The second problem is the fact that the education system is highly exam-oriented, which encourages teachers to make their classes very grammar-focused and therefore perceived by the students as not very relevant to real life.

Avoid informal words and phrases

The table below lists words and phrases that students sometimes use in their essays but that are too informal and/or vague for academic writing; do not use them.

Words and phrases that are too informal for academic writing			
Imprecise, incomplete or lazy	**Too emotional, subjective or informal**	**Redundant or meaningless**	**Sayings or clichés**

a bit
and so forth
and so on
etc.
sort of
stuff
thing
	awful
	besides
	incredible
	it's a great way of
	it's all too much
	it's just not on
	it's so hard
	it's such hard work
	it's unfair that
	meanwhile
	obvious
	pretty (meaning 'very')
	really and truly
	surely
	terrible
		after all
		along the way
		anyway
		at the end of
		  the day
		basically
		it all comes
		  down to
		the thing is
		when it comes
		  down to it
			in a nutshell
			last but not
			  least
			no one is
			  perfect
			to name but a
			  few
			to put it mildly

Over to You 23
Improve the style of these sentences

Improve the style of these sentences by replacing the informal words or phrases and/or rewriting the sentences. Suggested answers can be found on p.188.

1   Globalisation is really bad for the planet.

2   Some companies behave unethically and this kind of thing must stop.

3   The issue will be sorted by the government.

4   Basically, there's no evidence that mobile phone use damages health.

5   It all comes down to whether or not you can regulate your emotions.

6   It's pretty obvious that companies need to pay more attention to business ethics.

7   It will not help us anyway.

8   There are different kinds of businesses private, public, non-profit making and so on.

9   It's a pretty big problem.

10 The most important thing to do is to reduce carbon emissions.

Avoid two-word verbs

Avoid using too many two-word verbs (called phrasal verbs) such as *make up*, *get round*, *go up*, *help out* and *find out*, because they are often too informal and imprecise for academic writing. Use more formal and precise one-word equivalents such as *compensate*, *avoid*, *increase*, *assist* and *discover*.

Avoid redundant words

Writing in a formal style and discussing complex ideas does *not* mean that you have to use as many 'long words' as possible. Aim to convey complex ideas with brevity, and avoid using words that are overly complicated or that merely repeat the previous word. For example:

absolutely essential ✗	essential ✓	past history ✗	history ✓
close proximity ✗	proximity ✓	revert back to ✗	revert to ✓
conclusive proof ✗	proof ✓	endeavours to ✗	tries to ✓
different varieties ✗	varieties ✓	fabricated in ✗	built in ✓
hard evidence ✗	evidence ✓	commence with ✗	start with ✓
join together ✗	join ✓	true facts ✗	facts ✓
or, alternatively ✗	alternatively ✓	utilised ✗	used ✓

Over to You 24
Write in a formal but clear style

The style of the paraphrase below is too informal for academic writing. Rewrite it in a more appropriate style, replacing the subject/verb phrases with nouns where possible and appropriate. A suggested answer can be found on p.188.

Paraphrase

Côté and Morgan showed that as they thought would happen, if you keep a tight lid on bad feelings, you will be pretty unhappy with your job and so you'll be more likely to think about leaving it. Their research results also say that basically, if you increase your happy emotions, you'll feel loads better about your job because you'll get on better at your place of work, and on top of this you'll get better responses from your workmates and customers.

Be precise

Any statements or claims you make in your writing need to be both specific and supported by evidence in some way. In the two practice activities below, the sentences are either too general, too simplified, not specific enough, unsupported or generally unclear. Improve or correct the sentences. Suggested answers can be found on p.189.

Over to You 25
Make these sentences more specific and/or supported

1 People in poor countries get lower wages.

2 Portable technology is used by everyone nowadays.

3   We all see writing as having one main purpose but in fact it has many different functions.

4   Everyone knows that drugs are addictive.

5   Some people think that euthanasia should be legal but the politicians disagree.

6   In the modern world abortion is accepted.

7   The majority of men gamble in their twenties.

8   There are hundreds of women attacked each year.

9   There is more demand for organ transplants than ever before.

10 The UK has an increasing number of drug users.

Over to You 26
Make the meaning of these sentences more clear

1   The Mediterranean which is the dirtiest sea in the world is caused by tourism.

2   I have chosen to discuss cloning because I want to put forward the major advance technology and why I consider cloning to be prohibited.

3   Cloning animals has been debated between scientists, politicians and the general public on how cloning has been treated and how they might clone humans.

4   The nephron has five main parts for the process to work.

5   Academic writing is a form of writing that students adapt to their work.

6   Personal writing is more of your own feelings.

7   This is a holiday development for the country.

8   Deoxygenated blood is pumped from the heart into the lungs and vice versa.

9   Luchens (2006) found that some children are allowed to watch violent films by their parents, and that they behave more aggressively after watching them.

10 The government hopes that legislation will protect the public so that the fatalities between 1988 and 2001 can be avoided.

D2

Re-expressing and referencing your reading

As we saw in Chapters B1–3, when re-expressing source material you should *not* try simply to 'translate' it by taking each word, phrase or sentence in turn and replacing them with your own. This will result in a poor paraphrase that not only lacks flow and integration into your own essay, but is also a form of plagiarism because you will only have changed the words, not the sentence pattern and overall information structure. In order to avoid this trap you need to be familiar with what your source says, to the extent that you can put it away and write your own independent re-expression of the ideas it contains; when you do this you will naturally use language structures that are different from the source text. However, it is also useful to be aware of techniques you can use, and this chapter looks at some ways you can use vocabulary, grammar and structure to help you re-express your source material in your own way.

Language and grammar techniques for re-expressing your reading

Six useful techniques are:

- changing or reversing the order of the information;
- using different words that have similar meanings to the original ones (synonyms);
- changing the word forms;
- changing the tense of verbs;
- changing the voice of verbs;
- changing the structure of sentences.

As an example of using these techniques, below is the text extract we looked at in Chapter B2 on p.67, followed by a good student paraphrase. This is followed by a table showing how the student used the techniques above to produce their paraphrase.

Source extract

> So far there is no clear evidence from health studies of a relation between mobile phone use and mortality or morbidity. Indeed, tantalising findings in humans include a speeding up of reaction time during exposure, particularly during behavioural tasks calling for attention and electrical brain activity changes during cognitive processes. It is not clear, however, whether these findings have any positive implications for health.
>
> Adapted from: Maier, M., Blakemore, C. and Koivisto, M. (2000) 'The health hazards of mobile phones', *British Medical Journal* 320(7245), pp.1288–1289.

Student paraphrase

Interesting study results suggest that using a mobile phone results in quicker reaction times to some tasks which require both changes in electrical brain activity and concentration (Maier et al. 2000). Although it has not been shown that this effect represents an actual benefit to health, there has equally been no hard data from any disease studies to suggest that mobile phones actually damage health (ibid.).

	Original text	**Student paraphrase**
Changing or reversing the order of the information	1 *no clear evidence* 2 *speeding up of reaction time* 3 *unclear about positive health*	2 *speeding up of reaction time* 3 *unclear about positive health* 1 *no clear evidence*
Using synonyms	*tantalising findings* *mortality and morbidity* *clear evidence*	*interesting results* *disease studies* *hard data*
Changing word forms	*mobile phone use*	*using a mobile phone*
Changing verb tense or voice	*there is no clear evidence of* (present simple)	*there has been no hard data* (present perfect)
Changing sentence structure		*Although, . . . there has . . .*

Over to You 27
Awareness of language techniques for paraphrasing

Read the source extract and paraphrase below. Look at whether and/or how the student has used the six techniques described above in their paraphrase. Answers can be found on p.190. You may also like to look again at the source extracts and paraphrases on pp.61–69 to see how the techniques have been used.

Source extract

. . .there is indeed considerable overlap between ethics and the law. In fact, the law is essentially an institutionalisation or codification of ethics into specific social rules, regulations, and proscriptions. Nevertheless, the two are not equivalent. . . .The law might be said to be a definition of the minimum acceptable standards of behaviour. However, many morally contestable issues, whether in business or elsewhere, are not explicitly covered by the law. . . . In one sense then, business ethics can be said to begin where the law ends. Business ethics is primarily concerned with those issues not covered by the law, or where there is no definite consensus on whether something is right or wrong.

Extracts from: Crane, A. and Matten, D. (2010)
Business Ethics, pp.5, 7.

Student paraphrase

It is important to emphasise here that business ethics is not synonymous with legality. Business ethics is mainly concerned with areas of conduct that are *not* specifically covered by law and that are therefore open to different interpretations, a fact that means a particular behaviour may be legal, albeit viewed as unethical (Crane and Matten 2010). There is some overlap between law and ethics, but legislation usually only regulates the lowest level of acceptable behaviour (ibid.).

Different ways of introducing and referring to your reading

You can use different ways of referring to your source material to suit different purposes in your essay. Note that you will usually need to use all three methods in one essay.

1 Referencing to emphasise the information

If when using a source in your essay, it is the information and ideas that are important to your argument rather than the author, you can integrate your source material by paraphrasing, summarising or quoting and only giving the in-text reference at the end. For example:

> Finally, there is a third and I think most significant development. This is that many organisations are now starting to position themselves so that they can use the emergent idea of circular business and consumption models to become market leaders in the new 'ethical solutions' market rather than the sale of produced goods or items (Change the World 2017).

You can also use the passive voice for this type of emphasis:

> It has been suggested that violent films have a negative effect on children's behaviour (Carlton 1999; Cyprian 2001).

> This idea of the interdependence of any business organisation is also supported by Shaw and Barry (2007), Green (1994), Fritzsche (2005) and Svensson and Wood (2008).

2 Emphasising both the research context and the information

If you wish to refer explicitly to the research in some way, for example to comment on how much research has been done, you should state this, but again only give the specific reference at the end of the sentence in round brackets. For example:

> Various research studies have indicated that job satisfaction is linked to regulating emotion (Côté and Morgan 2002, Barrick 2002).

Note that this technique is useful for bringing together similar research or work.

3 Emphasising the author

If you wish to emphasise the specific author/s of the source, use the author as the subject of your sentence with only the year of publication in round brackets (or a number after the author's name for numeric referencing). For example:

> Trevino and Nelson (2010) point out that a perception that an organisation is behaving well will increase its attractiveness and thereby its stakeholder commitment.

You can use this method when you want to show that you have reviewed the literature and that you know who the key authors are, and which of them hold similar views to each other. For example:

> Svensson and Wood (2008) show that the two are in fact mutually dependent . . . Others such as Wolf (2008) share this view, and Prindl and Prodham (1994) suggest that . . .

Over to You 28
Write a paraphrase

Read the text extract below a couple of times and make some notes. When you are sure that you understand the extract properly and can use your understanding and notes to write a paraphrase, do this using your own words and style, using some of the language techniques and referencing methods described in this chapter. An example paraphrase can be found on p.191.

Source extract

Every day, in every industrialised country of the world, journalists and politicians give out a conscious and unconscious message. It is that better economic performance means more happiness for a nation. This idea is rarely questioned. We feel we would be more cheery if our boss raised our pay, and assume that countries must be roughly the same. The results in this paper suggest that, in a developed nation, economic progress buys only a small amount of extra happiness.

> Extract from: Oswald, A. J. (1997) 'Happiness and economic performance', *Economic Journal* 107(445), pp.1815–1831.

D3

Checking your referencing

The two most important aspects of using source material are firstly, to use it in an intelligent, critical and fair manner, and secondly, to make it easy for your reader to see when you are using it. In-text references and reference reminder phrases that show clearly all the switches between you and your source material are vital, and we have looked at how to do this in Part B of this book. The smaller more 'surface' aspects of referencing (such as punctuation and font type) are much less important, and getting these right does not necessarily mean that you are referencing effectively. However, you might still lose a few marks if you make a lot of mistakes with referencing technicalities, and so this chapter contains examples of student writing that contain such errors, to help you develop your awareness and skill in checking and correcting your own work. The sentences use a Harvard referencing style, the basic rules of which are:

● use the author's surname;
● if the author is the subject of your sentence, put only the year in round brackets;
● if the author is not the subject of your sentence, put both the name and year in round brackets.

Below are six practice activities, each one looking at a different aspect of in-text referencing. Identify the mistake or mistakes in each sentence and correct them if you can. Answers and comments can be found on pp.191–192.

Over to You 29
Correct the mistakes when referring to the author

1　According to (Dr Reynolds 2000) there is no strong evidence of long-term damage to health.

2　According to Dr Padash 2000 there is no strong evidence of long-term damage to health.

3　Georges Marchais (1984) discusses three main factors.

4 'Locke and Jimenez' show that early pre-school learning improves children's ability to process information.

5 **Folour and Skipton** (1991) found a strong correlation between amount of exposure to sunlight and depression.

6 Smith's article entitled location and personal identity, demonstrates how closely the two are related.

Over to You 30
Correct the mistake when referring to the source

1 'Global warming is a factual truth' (Greenpeace article).

2 A strong economy relies on moderate taxation methods (Sloman, Economics 3rd Edition).

3 These factors can be seen in the article titled 'Biometric data of the future'.

4 The website has drawn attention to the fact that more research needs to be done.

5 Locke (97) suggests that we need more evidence.

6 Smoking and related illness causes over 500,000 deaths annually in the UK.

Using *according to, quote, cite* or *source*

The two main points to note are:

- you should not usually use these words when referring to your own actions, only when you are stating that one author has cited or quoted another;
- you should not normally talk about the process you went through for researching and reading sources for your essay unless you are specifically asked to do so, for example in an assignment asking you to reflect on your research process.

Over to You 31
Correct the mistakes when using *according to*, *quote*, *cite* or *source*

1 According to me, the issue of global warming is not as serious as the media portrays.

2 Kerlinger (1969) quotes that: '*Science* is a misused and misunderstood word' (p. 1127).

3 From the published book written by Jones (2002) we can see that governments need to address this issue urgently.

4 As Collins (1994) cites, 'good ethics is synonymous with good management' (p. 2).

5 These factors are discussed in the source 'Dying to be thin'.

6 After researching many sources and reading eight articles over the last two weeks, I have found that the issue of global warming is controversial.

Mistakes with sentence grammar

Three useful points to remember here are:

● when you are giving a reference, the grammar needs to make sense, just as with any other sentence – the only difference is that sometimes you will be using the author's name as the main subject;

● if you do use the author or book/article title as the subject of your sentence, do not also use *it* / *they* / *their research*, as this would mean that your sentence contained two subjects for one verb;

● if you use the structure *As X states* / *shows* / *demonstrates,* do not use *that* after the verb.

Over to You 32
Correct the mistakes in sentence grammar

1 Côté and Morgan (2002) their research showed that emotion regulation affects job satisfaction.

2 Coates and Bailey (1995) their study examined three main aspects of mental health.

3 According to the *New Scientist* (8/1/2005), it states that people are still not aware of the effects the use of mobile phones can have.

4 As Crème and Lea (1997) have stated, that the gap between academic and personal writing is not as far apart as we assume.

5 Carr (1968) the analogy of a poker game to explain his point.

6 According to Smith (2000) states that the problem is widespread.

Mistakes with grammar and punctuation when using quotations

(See also Chapter B1, pp.55–59 for relevant practice activities.)

Over to You 33
Correct the mistakes in grammar and punctuation

1 In addition to this, 'effects on memory and attention and how microwaves alter electrical activity on the brain' will also be studied". (*New Scientist* (2005)))

2 The Body Shop, which for many years has branded itself as 'different because of our values' and which currently has an 'enrich not exploit' commitment policy. (The Body Shop 2018).

3 Knowles (1998) 'It has to be stated that groups work more efficiently' (p. 64).

4 Jones 2006 'importance of understanding the causes of mental ill health' (p. 12).

5 According to the *New Scientist* (8/1/2005), it states that 'although we all use mobile phones, most of us still don't know about the possible physical or mental effects this might have.

6 As Trevino and Nelson (2010) state Ethics is not just about the connection we have to other beings – we are all connected; rather, it's about the quality of that connection' (p. 32).

Checking your grammar

You will almost certainly need to make revisions to the content and organisation of your draft essay. You will also need to improve the organisation and style to suit your reader, a process referred to as editing. Once you have done this, you will probably need to read your draft essay again to check that each sentence makes sense, and to correct smaller points of grammar and punctuation; in other words, to proofread your work.

The occasional grammatical error will not matter too much, but making lots of mistakes will reduce the clarity and overall standard of your writing. If you find you are making mistakes in only a few grammatical areas but doing so repeatedly, it's probably worth revising the rules for these points so that you can get them right and improve the general accuracy of your language.

This chapter gives you brief explanations and examples for 16 grammatical areas that are common causes of error (you may also need to do some further grammar revision and practice of your own). Each point is followed by a short practice activity, and the chapter ends with some useful proofreading tips.

The points covered are listed below.

1 Incomplete sentences
2 Clauses that need separating
3 Confusing sentence pattern
4 Confusing tense changes
5 Unclear pronouns (*it, they, this* or *these*)
6 Subject–verb agreement (*have* or *has*?)
7 Use of the definite article (*the* or nothing?)
8 Prepositions (*in, at* or *on*?)
9 Infinitive and gerund (*to find* or *finding*?)
10 Word form (*important* or *importance*?)
11 Use of *that*
12 Commas with *that*
13 *Which, who* and *that* for essential information
14 *Which, who* and *that* for extra information
15 Apostrophes
16 Question marks

1 Incomplete sentences

A clause is a group of words that has at least a subject and a verb. Some clauses also form a complete thought and so can stand alone; these are called independent clauses. You can turn an independent clause into a sentence by putting a capital letter at the start and a full stop at the end. For example:

Wolf claims businesses should only be concerned with profit.

A clause that starts with a subordinating conjunction (e.g. *after, although, as, because, if, even if, since, though, whereas, while*), a relative pronoun (e.g. *which, who, that*) or a relative adverb (*when, where, why*) is called a subordinate or dependent clause, and cannot stand alone – it needs a second, independent clause to make sense and form a complete sentence. For example:

Whereas Wolf claims businesses should only be concerned with profit. ✗

Whereas Wolf claims businesses should only be concerned with profit, Trevino and Nelson (2010) argue that organisations also need to be socially responsible. ✓

Wolf claims businesses should only be concerned with profit, whereas Trevino and Nelson (2010) argue that organisations also need to be socially responsible. ✓

An error students sometimes make is to try to use only a dependent clause as a sentence, producing an incomplete (or fragment) sentence that does not make sense.

Over to You 34
Which sentences are incomplete?

1 Although there are several advantages.

2 Our data, which show a direct correlation between lack of light and depression, are flawed.

3 As they have found that it contains several inconsistencies.

4 As well as giving out benefits to families in poverty.

5 Because of fears about media attention, the defendant has not been named.

Missing verbs

All clauses, whether independent or dependent, need at least a subject and a main verb. Another common type of incomplete, fragment sentence is one in which the subject and/or main verb is missing.

Over to You 35
Add the missing subject and/or verb

1 An increasing number of people difficult to get a job.

2 Guideline daily amounts on food labels an alternative to the traffic light system of labelling.

3 Although a business needs to be seen as ethical now more than ever, we still cannot assume that it really is ethically.

4 The majority of drug users aged between eighteen and thirty.

5 The study of business ethics also important because it provides an informed framework.

2 Clauses that need separating

If you join two independent clauses (clauses that can stand alone) you need to have a linking word between them. Note that separating two independent clauses using only a comma is not enough. For example:

We conducted the experiment twice we found no long-term effects. ✗

We conducted the experiment twice, we found no long-term effects. ✗

We conducted the experiment twice, **and** (we) found no long-term effects. ✓

Note that if you join two independent clauses using *and, but, for, nor, so, or* or *yet* you need to put a comma before the linking word. If you want to use a conjunctive adverb such as *furthermore, however, nevertheless* or *moreover*, you need to make two separate sentences by using either a semi-colon or a full-stop (using a full-stop is increasingly acceptable) before the conjunctive and a comma afterwards. For example:

We conducted the experiment twice, but we found no long-term effects. ✓

We conducted the experiment twice; however, we were not able to duplicate the results. ✓

We conducted the experiment twice. However, we were not able to duplicate the results. ✓

Take particular care to make sure that you use a comma before *and, but, for, nor, so, or* or *yet* if you are linking two longer independent clauses so that the meaning of the whole sentence is clear to your reader. For example:

We conducted the same experiment as the teams in Paris and Vilnius had done, **and** we found that there were no long-term effects. ✓

If both parts of the sentence are very complex, you should think about splitting it into two sentences. For example:

> We conducted the same experiment to the same specifications as the teams in Paris and Vilnius had done in the previous two tests, and we found that contrary to the expectations we discussed in our previous paper, there were no long-term effects. ✓

> We conducted the same experiment to the same specifications as the teams in Paris and Vilnius had done in the previous two tests. We found that contrary to the expectations we discussed in our previous paper, there were no long-term effects. ✓

Over to You 36
Improve these sentences

1   Côté and Morgan have shown that emotion regulation influences job satisfaction and that amplifying positive emotions increases positive interaction with both colleagues and customers but that there is not an opposite correlation, that is, that job satisfaction affects emotion regulation.

2   The business decisions managers take can have significant implications, most managers do not have training in business ethics.

3   The World Wide Web is a constantly developing technology, it has many advantages for society.

4   Lupton (1998) claims that the public is interested in health news, however, I will argue that media coverage does not indicate genuine public interest.

5   Wolf (2008) argues that business should not concern itself with social consequences, on the other hand, Svensson and Wood claim that business and society are co-dependent.

3 Confusing sentence pattern

You should use a consistent grammatical pattern to express two or more ideas that are linked to the same thing in a sentence. Changing the grammatical structure of the components in such 'lists' will make your sentence difficult to understand. For example:

Leibens (2018) looks at the stages of **initiating** a project, **how to plan** and **closure**. ✗

                                gerund phrase   *how* phrase   noun

Leibens (2018) looks at the stages of **initiating**, **planning** and **closing** a project. ✓

                                gerund   gerund   gerund phrase

Leibens (2018) looks at the stages of project **initiation, planning*** and **closure.** ✓

noun   noun   noun

(*planning is both the gerund and noun form)

Over to You 37
Improve these sentences

1 Collins (1994) suggests that if businesses do not operate with a degree of trust and co-operating inside the organisation, they will put constraints on profitability.

2 What the 2017 World Happiness Report suggests is that people need to feel that they have social support, being able to make choices, and that they can trust national institutions.

3 Our survey revealed that students generally find journal articles more difficult than listening to lectures.

4 Skrzypiec (2017) uses the ITT model to test how important drugs, fighting and having stolen things are as factors in adolescents' intention to transgress.

5 Having good neighbours, socialising and available help are all key factors in community support for the elderly (Liu 2016).

4 Confusing tense changes

We usually use the present simple tense to discuss what sources say, because the research and ideas are still relevant, even though they were published in the past. For example:

> Geizen (2012) **states** that it is important to keep a megaproject as simple as possible.

> Research **shows** that public participation in land use policy benefits all parties (Booth and Halseth, 2011; Fraser et al., 2006).

> Various studies **show** that public participation in land use policy benefits all parties (Booth and Halseth, 2011; Fraser et al., 2006).

You can also use the present perfect simple in the above examples, but the present perfect is more commonly used to discuss research that you are putting into a wider context, particularly when you are then going on to discuss other more recent work and/or your own current research. The present perfect tense is therefore often used to group sources in a literature review. For example:

> Various studies **have shown** that public participation in land use policy benefits all parties (Booth and Halseth, 2011; Fraser et al., 2006), and our research takes this idea a step further.

You can use the past simple to discuss sources when you are putting them in a specific historical context, and/or when showing how they compare to more recent and current research (usually referred to in the present perfect or present simple tense). For example:

> In 1985 Sowell **stated** that Marx's ideas were 'a mighty instrument for the acquisition and maintenance of political power' (Sowell 1985, p.218).

> Newton's theory of gravity **was proved** incorrect by Einstein, and despite recent developments in quantum mechanics, Einstein's theories of relativity **have** so far **proved** infallible.

The important thing is not to change tense for no particular reason, as this will confuse your reader. For example:

> Chirenje et al. (2013) **are** in favour of public participation, but others such as Cornwall and Brock (2005) **argued** that this did not work. ✗

Over to You 38
Improve these sentences

1 Wolf (2008) shares this view and Prindle (2009) also suggested that . . .

2 The solution was put into the test tube and has been heated to 90 degrees.

3 If this theory were correct, it will mean that all previous data . . .

4 Ariti et al. (2018) have argued that farmer participation increases ownership and they also suggested that it helps social cohesion.

5 Geizen (2012) is stating that it is important to keep a megaproject as simple as possible.

5 Unclear pronouns

Personal pronouns (e.g. *she, he, it*), possessive pronouns (e.g. *hers, his, its*), and demonstrative pronouns (*this, that, these, those*) are useful in academic writing. However, a common mistake is to use a pronoun to refer back to something in a previous phrase or sentence that has several nouns, making the meaning of the pronoun unclear. Moreover, a reader will normally assume that a pronoun refers to the noun immediately preceding it, and so if you use a pronoun to refer to an earlier noun, again, your meaning will not be clear. For example, in the two essay extracts below we are not sure which noun or phrase (in bold) *it* and *this* refer to:

Both **the report** and **subsequent data** have revealed **a lack of knowledge** about dietary supplements among young people. <u>**It**</u> was discussed among all political parties and a national debate is now under way. ✗

At **the conference, which cost over £1million to hold**, representatives from the six countries had **a heated debate** about how to balance **economic development** with **sustainable use of resources**. <u>**This**</u> is causing increasing controversy and is likely to derail next year's summit. ✗

In each extract the meaning needs to be clarified by either repeating the relevant noun or phrase from the first sentence, or by using an equivalent noun (so as to avoid repetition), rather than using a pronoun:

Both the report and subsequent data have revealed a lack of knowledge about dietary supplements among young people. <u>**The report**</u> was discussed among all political parties and a national debate is now under way. ✓

At the conference, which cost over £1million to hold, representatives from the six countries had a heated debate about how to balance economic development with sustainable use of resources. <u>**This issue of how to maintain both growth and sustainability**</u> is causing increasing controversy and is likely to derail next year's summit. ✓

Over to You 39
Improve these sentences

1   According to Giezen's model, in a megaproject the probability of budget overrun can often be reduced by keeping it as simple as possible (Giezen M., 2012).

2   Players and team coaches were classified according to sport and to the number of games they currently played each season.

3   The city's transport policy will lead to an increase in traffic, which will be detrimental to local air quality and noise pollution. This is the most important thing to consider at this meeting.

4   If these personal road accident stories are shared, they will hopefully be reduced.

5   The 2018 report is a key document, showing the importance of job satisfaction, and it needs to be taken seriously by both businesses and governments.

6 Subject–verb agreement (*have* or *has*?)

In the present simple tense the third-person singular (e.g. *she, it, the essay*) takes a regular verb form that ends in *s*.

Third-person singular (present simple tense)	
Subject	**Verb**
For example: he / she / it / Smith / the book / the article / the author / the report / the experiment / the issue / the debate / the essay / the experiment / the finding / the project / the researcher / the result / the statistic / the study / the theory	For example: Regular verbs: argues / involves / shows / suggests / reports To be: is To have: **has**

Confusingly perhaps, the plural subjects (*we* and *they*) do *not* have an s at the end of the verb.

Plural (present simple tense)	
Subject	**Verb**
For example: we / they / you / the books / the authors / the issues / the results / the research projects	For example: Regular verbs: argue / involve / show / suggest / report To be: are To have: have

Uncountable nouns

These are nouns that are usually treated as singular, and so take the third-person singular verb form (+ s). Uncountable nouns include abstract nouns, which are common in academic writing.

The names of academic disciplines are also uncountable (even though some of them end in an s). For example: *economics, genetics, linguistics, mathematics.*

Uncountable nouns as third-person singular subject (present simple tense)	
Subject	**Verb**
For example: information / importance / energy / equipment / evidence / importance / information / knowledge / progress / proof / research / technology / business / mathematics	For example: Regular verbs: argues / involves / shows / suggests / reports To be: is To have: **has**

Making uncountable nouns countable

To count an uncountable noun you need to use it together with a countable one. For example:

Uncountable noun	Uncountable + countable noun
The evidence suggest**s**	A piece of evidence that suggest**s**
	Three piece**s** of evidence suggest
This knowledge show**s**	This aspect of knowledge show**s**
	These aspect**s** of knowledge show
The research involve**s**	The research project involve**s**
	Both research project**s** involve
Technology **is** now	This type of technology **is** now
	Different type**s** of technology are

Subject–verb agreement for some common phrases

Phrases that use the third-person singular verb form (verb + s)

It is <u>either</u> the first <u>or</u> the second experiment that **needs** to be repeated.

<u>Neither</u> Wolf <u>nor</u> Carr **suggests** that businesses should concern themselves with ethics.

<u>Everyone / anyone / someone /no one</u> **understands** that . . .

<u>Another</u> problem **is** . . .

<u>The</u> (total) <u>number of</u> cases **is** not significant.

<u>The total</u> of 120 **is** higher than expected.

<u>The average</u> age **is** . . .

<u>A</u> large / small / significant <u>amount of</u> work **has** been done on this topic.

Phrases that use the plural verb form (verb + no s)

Other issue<u>s</u> also **need** to be examined.

There **are** <u>many</u> project**s** / There **are** <u>few</u> studies.

<u>A</u> (large / small / significant) <u>number of</u> patient**s** **have** recovered.

Phrases that can use the third-person singular *or* plural subject

If the first noun in the sentence is a fraction, percentage or proportion, the verb should agree with the noun closest to it. For example:

The majority / 60% / two-thirds / a quarter of <u>the journal</u> **contains** articles on DLV theory.

The majority / a minority /60% / two-thirds / a quarter of <u>the responses</u> **contain** errors.

157

Over to You 40
Improve these sentences

1 Smith et al. (2000) reports that this level of violence is harmful.

2 Recent research also show that the drugs are effective.

3 Malicious software such as worms have been increasingly used.

4 The two types differs in the way they can be treated.

5 A research company have recently produced a new report.

7 Use of the definite article (*the* or nothing?)

Two common mistakes are either to use *the* (called the definite article) where there should be nothing, or to have nothing where there should be *the*. Below are brief examples to remind you of the basic rules.

Nothing

Uncountable nouns used in a general way

Progress has been made

Evidence is needed to support a claim

Research into cancer has increased

Metal is generally a good conductor of electricity

Information is only as reliable as the source

Economics and psychology are both very broad disciplines

Society needs laws

Countable plural nouns used in a general way

People are complex

Experiments need to be reliable

Academic journals are useful

Research projects always need funding

Proper nouns (names)

Smith (2000) discusses only a few aspects of this research

Einstein proposed his general theory of relativity in 1915

I will argue that Freud had no scientific basis for his theory of mind

Possessive forms of proper nouns

Smith's research

Einstein's theory

Freud's ideas

Names of diseases

Influenza has several different strains

Cases of measles have risen sharply

The

Uncountable nouns used in a specific way

The team's progress has been good

The evidence given in court was unreliable

The research in this study needs to be repeated

The metal used in the prototype is too expensive

The information given in the report is accurate

The psychology textbook is only appropriate for first-year students

The society of today is very different from that of our parents

Countable plural nouns used in a specific way

The people at the conference

The experiments mentioned earlier in the report

The academic journals used in the essay

The research projects completed last year now need to be written up

When only one exists

The nuclear transfer method

The immune system

The organic method

When it is clear which one is being referred to

Ordinals: The first / The second / The last

Superlatives: The least / The most / The best / The highest / The most recent

Specifiers: The main factor / The principal issue / The essential / The only / The same

Something already introduced: Kahil conducted a study last year. The research suggested that . . .

When referring to all things defined by the noun

The average brain contains about 100 million neurons

The computer is now the most important technological device that exists

The methodology section in a dissertation should explain how data was collected

Part of a whole

None of the / All of the / Some of the / Most of the / Half of the / 60% of the

Names used as adjectives

The Freudian theory of psychosis

Over to You 41
Improve these sentences

1   Marx argued for fundamental changes in the society.

2   It is expected that public will benefit from this technology.

3   Third disadvantage is that it is expensive.

4   For majority of people, mobile phones are now almost indispensable.

5   The study shows that immune system is extremely complex.

8 Prepositions (*in, at* or *on?*)

Prepositions (e.g. *in, at, on, by, for, under, over, through, between, during*) describe the relationship between two things in either time or space. For example:

Research in the field of quantum mechanics

Research at the hospital

Research on nuclear physics

Research by Jones

Research for the government

Research conducted under Dr Patel

Check that you have used the correct prepositions. Use a dictionary to give you information on this, and also take note of preposition phrases you come across as you read.

Over to You 42
Improve these sentences

1 Patel states that we developed music before language (Patel 2000, cited from Bragg 2003).

2 Prevention for type 1 diabetes is not possible.

3 They are both at a constant state of balance.

4 The negative effects on using genetically modified crops are listed below.

5 The materials used were pertinent of the experiment.

9 Infinitive and gerund (*to find or finding?*)

Some verbs are usually followed by the infinitive (to + v.), some by an object + infinitive, and a few verbs, for example *have, leave and prepare*, can be followed by either of these structures. Other verbs are followed by a gerund (v. + ing) and others by a preposition + gerund.

A good dictionary should provide you with example sentences that show you what type of structure usually follows a particular verb, and you can also take note of such phrases when you are reading. Lists of some useful verbs and the structures that commonly follow them are given below.

Verb + infinitive

We **attempt to prove**

They **failed to accept**

They **expect to find**

They **neglect to show**

Verb + object + infinitive

We **allowed the patients to go** home.

Kajinsky (2016) **challenges Procter to find** evidence of this claim.

The aim of the advert is to **persuade its consumers to buy** more paper books.

The research **requires further scrutiny to determine** the real cause.

Verb + gerund

We **advise investigating** the problem.

Our team **considered repeating** the experiment.

The report **suggests raising** the quota.

The company **risks losing** its main supplier if it does not lower its prices.

Verb + preposition + gerund

No institution has **admitted to covering** up the scandal.

Our recommendation is that the company **concentrates on increasing** productivity.

Whether or not the vaccine works **depends on administering** it within 12 hours of infection.

The campaign **succeeded in discouraging** voters from going to the polls.

Over to You 43
Improve these sentences

1   The model is capable to make accurate predictions.

2   The increase in greenhouse gases causes the temperature rising.

3   We discussed about increase the number of employees.

4   The failure of cells from removing sugars causes diabetes.

5   Lewes (2000) rejects the idea to use DNA as evidence of guilt.

10 Word form (*important* or *importance*?)

Using the wrong form of a word (e.g. *creative* instead of *creativity*) can be confusing for your reader and can prevent you from conveying your meaning clearly. For example:

Knowles (2000) **difference** between the theory and practice of primary education. ✗

The amount of planning needed is not **equally** at all stages of a project. ✗

The contract specified **restricting of** time and cost. ✗

I have **demonstration** that business and society are interdependent. ✗

Knowles (2000) **differentiates** between the theory and practice of primary education. ✓

The amount of planning needed is not **equal** at all stages of a project. ✓

The contract specified **restrictions** of time and cost. ✓

I have **demonstrated** that business and society are interdependent. ✓

Use a dictionary to give you information and examples of which form of a word to use, and see also Appendix 4 on p.199. Be aware that individual words in a word family sometimes have different meanings. For example, *a conclusion* means 'the end of something' but *conclusive* means 'definite and decisive'.

Over to You 44
Improve these sentences

1   The consultation process should continuous to the final stage of the project.

2   The 2018 report will make an important contributing to the government's strategy.

3   The article clear states that more research needs to be conducted.

4   Conclusively, this essay has shown that this question needs further investigation.

5   There is still a potentially market for buy-to-let construction developments.

11 Use of *that*

that + no comma

Students sometimes mistakenly put a comma before or after *that*. Nearly all sentences and phrases with *that* do **not** have commas. This rule also applies to using *that* when introducing a quotation or paraphrase. For example:

> Prindl and Prodham (1994) state that 'Finance as practiced in the professions . . .'

> The evidence suggests that ageism is partly unconscious.

> It seems / appears / is clear that a strong correlation exists.

> It is important that we consider the report in detail.

> The fact is that the war did not help the country.

> The results were so surprising that they were not believed at first.

> There is only one issue that is really problematic.

> That is a situation I find hard to imagine.

> The experiment that was conducted by Smith's team provided useful data.

> The authors that disagree with Carr are Esty and Collins.

that + comma

The only time *that* uses a comma is in the phrase 'that is' meaning 'namely'. Here you need to use a comma both before and after *that is*. For example:

> There is one problematic issue, that is, the effect of the reservoir on the local environment.

Compare the two uses of *that* in the example below:

> There is only one issue **that** needs to be discussed, **that is**, how best to use our resources.

Over to You 45
Improve these sentences

1   It has been shown in this essay that, this is not the case.

2   It is illogical, that people think pollution is not important.

3   The fact is that, we cannot determine the outcome.

4   This essay will discuss the most important aspect of genetic research that is cloning.

5   Lenin (1914) claimed that, a nation could not be truly free while it oppressed other nations.

12 *Which, who* and *that* for essential information

Essential information clauses = no commas

If the *which* or *who* part of your sentence is essential for identifying which thing is being talked about (called an identifying, defining or restrictive clause) you should not put a comma before *which* or at the end of the *which* clause. In the examples below the *which* and *who* clauses identify which experiment, team and authors are being discussed.

Although most of the research was inconclusive, the experiment **which Smith's team conducted** has provided useful data.

Although most of the research was inconclusive, the experiment **which was conducted by Smith's team** has provided useful data.

The team **who conducted the first study** showed that their data were the most significant.

The authors **who disagree with Carr** are Esty and Collins.

Using *that* instead of *which* or *who*

In an identifying clause you can use *that* instead of *which* or *who*:

Although most of the research was inconclusive, the experiment **that Smith's team conducted** provided useful data.

Although most of the research was inconclusive, the experiment **that was conducted by Smith's team** provided useful data.

The team **that conducted the first study** showed that their data were the most significant.

The authors **that disagree with Carr** are Esty and Collins.

Omitting *which, who* or *that*

You can leave out the relative pronoun *which, who* or *that* if it refers to the object in the clause (e.g. the experiment):

…, the experiment **Smith's team conducted** provided useful data. ✓

… , the experiment **conducted by Smith's team** provided useful data. ✓

Note that if the verb is in the passive voice you also need to leave out the 'to be' part of the passive verb:

> … ,the experiment **was conducted by Smith's team** provided useful data. ✗

> … ,the experiment **conducted by Smith's team** provided useful data. ✓

If the relative pronoun of the identifying clause refers to the subject in the clause (e.g. the team, the authors), you cannot leave it out:

> The team **conducted the first study** showed that their data was the most significant. ✗

> The authors **disagree with Carr** are Esty and Collins. ✗

> The team **which / that conducted the first study** showed that their data was the most significant. ✓

> The authors **who / that disagree with Carr** are Esty and Collins. ✓

Over to you 46
Improve these sentences

1   The study relevant to the debate is the one, which is presented, in Jacobs's 2017 paper.

2   The patients in the survey experienced side-effects were taken out of the trial.

3   The company director oversaw the project has written a book about her experience.

4   Out of the range of options many commentators have suggested the system, which allows different states to have autonomy would be best.

5   The factors, that might affect the way a text is written are listed below.

13 *Which, who* and *that* for extra information

Extra information clauses = comma at each end

If the *which* or *who* part of your sentence is not needed to identify what is being talked about, and could therefore be left out of the sentence, you need to put a comma at each end. This type of clause is called a non-identifying, non-defining or non-restrictive clause. For example:

> Business ethics, **which has become increasingly important**, can be defined as principles of behaviour as applied to business organisations.

Svensson and Wood, **who disagree with Carr,** propose a dynamic model of business ethics.

With an extra information clause you cannot replace *which* or *who* with *that* and you cannot leave out the pronoun. For example:

Business ethics, **that has become increasingly important,** can be defined as principles of behaviour as applied to business organisations. ✗

Business ethics, **has become increasingly important,** can be defined as principles of behaviour as applied to business organisations. ✗

Svensson and Wood, **that disagree with Carr,** propose a dynamic model of business ethics. ✗

Svensson and Wood, **disagree with Carr,** propose a dynamic model of business ethics. ✗

Over to You 47
Improve these sentences

1   The article summarised above, contradicts my own data has not been peer reviewed.

2   Social media, that is now a common publishing platform, challenges the concept of 'facts'.

3   Jacobs's data which is summarised below in Figure 3 is the most relevant to the current debate.

4   Jacobs's data is summarised below in Figure 3 is the most relevant to the current debate.

5   Stockieve's theory has been used to justify violence which was not his intention.

14 Apostrophes

You should not use contractions in formal writing (*do not* > *don't, they are* > *they're, it is/has* > *it's, who is* > *who's*), and so there should only be one reason to use an apostrophe in your essays, that is, to show possession. Below are lists of examples to remind you of how and when to use apostrophes and *s* to show possession.

Singular noun > 's

For example: The research **of Patel**   > **Patel's** research

Teams from **this country**   > **This country's** teams

This rule applies even when the noun already ends with an *s*.

For example: The research **of Kimos**   > **Kimos's** research

The population **of Cyprus**   > **Cyprus's** population

Nowadays it is sometimes acceptable to omit the second *s* but it is never wrong to use it.

Plural noun that ends in *s* > *s'*

For example: The theories of **the authors**   > **The authors'** theories

The responses of **the students**   > **The students'** responses

Plural noun that does <u>not</u> end in an *s* > 's

For example: The group belonging to **the women**   > **The women's** group

The charter belonging to **the people**   > **The people's** charter

Its

Although we use apostrophes to show possession (including *anyone's*, *anybody's*, *everyone's*, *someone's* and *one's*) we do <u>not</u> use them for the possessive personal pronouns – *mine, yours, his, hers, its, ours* and *theirs*.

For example: The title of the article is too long.   > It's title is too long. ✗

Its title is too long. ✓

Over to You 48
Improve these sentences

1   Some theologist's think that therapeutic cloning is acceptable.

2   Greenpeace states that one of it's aims is to expose threats to the environment.

3   A countries government usually resides in the capital city.

4   An employees career is influenced by many different factors.

5   We analysed the students's questionnaires using this universitys' own software programme.

15 Question marks

Direct questions use a question word order and end with a question mark.

Indirect questions do not have a question mark at the end. They have an introductory phrase indicating that a question is being asked (e.g. *The question is whether*), followed by a second clause that has a non-question word order.

Direct question	Indirect question
What is the key issue in the campaign?	We need to ask **what** the key issue in the campaign **is**.
Can mobile phones **cause** illness?	The question is **whether** mobile phones **can cause** illness.
What has this research **achieved**?	It is unclear **what** this research **has achieved**.

Common mistakes students make when using direct and indirect questions are:

● **using too many direct questions**

Direct questions are a little informal for academic writing and so should be used sparingly.

● **using an indirect question with the word order of a direct question**

For example: It is unclear what **has** this research achieved. ✗
It is unclear what this research **has** achieved. ✓

● **using a question mark with an indirect question.**

For example: We need to ask what the key issue in the campaign is? ✗
We need to ask what the key issue in the campaign is. ✓

Over to You 49
Improve these sentences

1   The question is whether mobile phones make us sick?

2   The issue is if this will lead to an increase in violence.

3   Research was conducted to see what was the cause of the disease.

4   It is unclear what is the problem with the strategy.

5   The question remains as to what has this research achieved.

Top tips for proofreading your work

Students who check their work carefully at least three or four times usually get higher marks for their work than those who re-read it only once or twice. So, proofread your work several times if possible, and use these tips to be more effective when you do so.

- Try to leave plenty of time for checking and correcting your work; re-reading and amending your assignment several times is a key part of the writing process, not something that should be left to the last minute.
- Remember that you must try to see what you have actually written rather than what you *think* you have written.
- Try printing out your essay and checking this paper version, rather than just looking at your work on screen. Reading a paper copy may help you to see your essay in a fresh and more objective way (almost as someone else's work) and so you will spot mistakes more easily.
- Try reading a paper version of your work slowly out loud. This can be an effective way of hearing mistakes you might not detect just by reading your work through in your mind.
- You can also try recording yourself reading your work and then playing back the recording so that you can hear whether your sentences make sense. Getting someone else to read out your work to you may also help you to hear what you have actually put on the page.
- Remember that the grammar and spellcheck on your computer will only detect a limited range of mistakes, and that these online tools are not an adequate substitute for your own careful checking and correcting.
- If possible, put your essay or report away for a few hours between each check.

The more you practise checking your writing, the better you will become at spotting mistakes and improving your writing generally, and being able to edit and proofread your work is an important skill for both university study and professional life.

Appendices

Appendix 1

Complete student essay on business ethics

Outline what business ethics is and discuss whether it is important (2,500 words)

Over the past couple of decades, the issue of the ethical stance of businesses appears to have become more explicitly an area of public debate and consumer awareness. Two illustrations of this are the number of publications that give consumers information about the most ethical companies (for example the Ethispere and Good Shopping Guide sites), and the fact that many large organisations now have an 'our ethics' tab somewhere on their website. The UK ethical sales market is currently valued at over £38 billion, and has been expanding year on year over the past decade, with current growth at about 8.5% (Ethical Consumer Research Association and Triodos Bank 2017). In this essay I will briefly define business ethics and then consider whether it does and should have value as an aspect of both business activity and business theory and training.

Defining what constitutes a business is contentious in itself, but for the purposes of this short essay I will define a business as any profit-making enterprise, including charities (who make profits to invest back into the enterprise). Similarly, there are numerous, overlapping definitions of business ethics. Shaw and Barry (2007) define it as 'what constitutes right and wrong (or good and bad) human conduct in a business context' (p. 25). This is a broad definition that needs some refining in two areas. One distinction to make is that ethics is not the same thing as general morality. Crane and Matten (2016) explain that although morals are a basic premise of ethics, ethics and ethical theory go a step further because they focus on how morals can be *applied* to produce explicit standards and rules for particular contexts, of which business is one. Ferrell, Fraedrich and Ferrell's definition of business ethics as the 'principles and standards that guide behaviour in the world of business' (Ferrell et al. 2002, p.6) is pertinent here, as it emphasises the application of morals to produce codes and guidelines. Codified ethical behaviour usually falls under what's called 'corporate social responsibility' (CSR), which in turn is usually seen as part of corporate governance, although there is overlap between the two areas of activity.

The second aspect of defining business ethics which needs unpacking is that, as Crane and Matten point out, ethics is not synonymous with legality. They state that there is some overlap between law and ethics, but that legislation usually only regulates the lowest level of acceptable behaviour. In addition, as Trevino and Nelson (2010) state, the law is limited in what it can do to prevent unacceptable actions, because legislation follows rather than precedes trends in behaviour. Business ethics, then, according to Crane and Matten, is mainly concerned with areas of conduct that are *not* specifically covered by law, and that are therefore open to different interpretations, a fact that means a particular behaviour may be legal albeit viewed by many as unethical.

Combining all the perspectives outlined above, I define business ethics as any aspect of business standards, guidelines or accepted organisational practice developed directly or indirectly from moral principles. Importantly, I will include in this definition of ethical behaviour actions that can be considered ethical, regardless of whether they arise from a genuine desire to be moral or merely as a result of profit-driven activities.

Views differ widely as to whether ethics have a valid place in business, ranging from a clear 'yes', and the argument that ethical behaviour should be a core value in any organisation, to a definite 'no', with the argument that ethics should not play any part in a business. Opponents of the concept of ethics in business include those who claim that making a profit is the only responsibility a business has to society (Friedman 1970, cited in Fisher and Lovell 2003). Others such as Wolf (2000) share this view, and Carr (1968) uses the analogy of a poker game to argue that a successful businessman needs to play by the rules of the industry and that these include 'bluffing' as an acceptable form of behaviour. He suggests that what is, in effect, lying is merely part of legitimate business strategy, and that business rules do not need to take account of personal or social principles. Similarly, Prindl and Prodham (1994) point out that 'Finance as practised in the professions and in industry is seen as a value-neutral positive discipline, promoting efficiency without regard to the social consequences which follow from its products' (p. 3).

In this essay I am going to argue against those who see business ethics as irrelevant, and suggest that on the contrary, ethics are essential to businesses for four interrelated and overlapping reasons; to operate and function successfully; to maintain sustained growth and profit; to fulfil legal and regulatory guidelines and requirements, and finally because of moral imperative – the fact that it is both logically and instinctively 'right' to behave ethically. I will argue that all four of these reasons for the relevance of business ethics are subsumed under one overriding rationale for ethical behaviour; that businesses are part of society, not separate from it.

The first of my four points, then, is that businesses actually need to behave in an ethical manner in order to function properly. This idea is supported by Fritzsche (2005) and expressed succinctly by Collins (1994) when he states that 'good ethics is synonymous with good management' (p. 2). Collins states that if managers only concern themselves with profit, they will become 'dysfunctional'. This is because any business is made up of people: employees, customers and other stakeholders. He suggests that if businesses do not operate with a degree of trust, co-operation and consideration both inside the organisation and externally, they will in fact be putting constraints on profitability.

A consideration of the impact on the outward-facing aspects of a business bring us to the second reason I give for the need of organisations to behave in an ethical manner, that of market growth and profit. Increasingly, various types of stakeholders (such as customers, governments and even some financial markets) want and expect businesses to behave well. This is particularly true for multinationals, whose activities involve the use of resources and employees in other countries. It is becoming more frequently the case that 'citizens of first world societies expect their corporations to display integrity in their international business dealings' (Svensson and Wood 2008, p. 312), and Trevino and Nelson (2010) state that a perception that an organisation is behaving well will increase its attractiveness and thereby its stakeholder commitment. Esty (2007) also notes that companies are now expected to publish reports on aspects of their activities such as greenhouse-gas emission and energy performance, and if they do not reach expected ethical targets, their reputation and possibly also their financial investment prospects are likely to suffer – a point that links back to the idea of businesses actually needing to be ethical to be profitable. In the world of instant global media, incidences of poor behaviour and exploitation are impossible to hide. Three recent and well-known examples of the damage such negative publicity can do are the ethically-themed scandals involving Starbucks, Nike and Primark. The websites of all three companies now devote a large amount of space to various corporate responsibility, sustainability and ethical standards monitoring reports, and to details of how they now have ethical conduct at the top of their agendas.

There are three interesting emergent business sectors that take the idea of consumer demand for ethical business a step further. Firstly, some organisations now base their core marketing and productions strategy on being ethical, The Body Shop being a prime example, which has for many years branded itself as 'different because of our values' and which now has an explicit commitment to ensuring that 'workplaces, and those of our main suppliers, are free from modern slavery, exploitation and discrimination' (The Body Shop 2018). The second significant development in taking ethical business to another level is that corporate social responsibility is now a growing market in its own right. The third most recent, and I think also most significant development, is the fact that many organisations are now starting to position themselves so that they can use global ethical discussions and the emergent idea of circular business and consumption models to become market leaders in finding innovative solutions to address sustainability, and so grow in the new 'ethical solutions' market rather than the sale of produced goods or items (*Fortune* 2017).

The third of the main reasons for which I suggest businesses need to behave well is that of regulatory and legal guidelines and requirements. Published guidelines and standards protocols have arisen as part of the international debates on corporate social responsibility, particularly in the areas of sustainability, climate change and workers' conditions. Important recent examples of these are the UN *Guiding Principles for Business and Human Rights* (Ruggie 2011), the UN's sustainable development goals (United Nations 2015), the Paris agreement on climate change (UNFCCC 2015) and the International Organisation for Standardisation's *Guidelines for Business Social and Ethical Responsibilities* (ISO 2010). In terms of legal compulsion, there is a wealth of legislation in areas such as working time, race relations, disability, employment and health and safety, which, if adhered to, force business entities to behave well. In addition, legislation such as the UK Companies Act 2006 and EU Accounts Modernisation Directive require directors to consider their organisation's environmental impact. The one area of business which is less regulated than others is the financial sector, but even financial markets have to adhere to the law most of the time.

We now come to my fourth argument for the necessity of business ethics – the question of whether they are relevant in the purely logical and moral sense, regardless of any other reasons. One could argue that this question does not have an objectively correct answer or truth. However, I think that it can be answered in the positive by the fact that all the various aspects of CSR and corporate governance already discussed are themselves manifestations of businesses existing in a society underpinned by a moral imperative. The relevance of the real-world moral imperative in business is arguably even more evident when we look at what happens when business entities do *not* behave ethically. The example I will use to illustrate this is doubly pertinent because it looks at the sector which is least regulated, and is therefore often perceived as most distant from instances of 'forced' good behaviour – the financial sector. The US financial crisis of 2008 occurred because four main factors combined to create global financial chaos: banks behaving unethically to borrowers (lending money they knew people could not repay) and creating unethical financial products (credit default swapping); an overly lax attitude from credit-rating agencies; unethical regulatory practices, and finally, 'ethical blindness' from boards of directors and risk assessors within the banks themselves (USS 2011). The chaos that ensued caused a global lack of confidence in the financial markets and helped hasten the European sovereign debt crisis. Whether this is because such crashes are an inherent part of free-market economics (as proposed in the European Commission's 2009 report) or that the unethical behaviour of the banks caused an atypical financial crisis (USS 2011), the 2008 crash had legal but nevertheless highly unethical business behaviour at its core. The profound and wide-ranging consequences of the crash affected both society and the sector that caused it, demonstrating (not for the first time) that the financial market is not somehow 'value-neutral'.

As I have stated, the four reasons I give for the relevance of business ethics all stem from the fact that organisations and society are interdependent. This idea is supported by Shaw and Barry (2007), Green (1994), Fritzsche (2005), Svensson and Wood (2008) and others. Svensson and Wood offer a model showing how business and society are mutually dependent and responsible for the consequences and effects of the other in a continuous and dynamic process. I would say that a practical manifestation of this idea is the fact that most major religions have something to say about how businesses should conduct themselves in society: Sharia banking law prohibits charging interest on loans; Confucian thought discourages profit-seeking; Christianity has the fundamental principle of treating others as you would have them treat you; and the influential philosophical approach of Kantianism sees the business firm as a 'moral community' (Bowie 2017), which links back to the idea of moral imperative.

So far I have looked at ethics as they relate to real-world business. I would now like to mention briefly the importance of business ethics as a tool for analysis, research, study and education. As already discussed, the power of organisations is increasing both nationally and globally, and the decisions business people make can have far-reaching effects. Despite this fact, managers surprisingly often have no specific training in ethics. I would argue that events such as the 2008 crash demonstrate that such training is badly needed, and that business ethics as a field of education and training within organisations is vital. Business ethics as a field of study and research is also important, because it provides an informed framework and source of criteria through which business behaviour can be analysed and evaluated by legal bodies and other groups in society. As Crouch (2011) states when discussing the political and financial power of multinational corporations, civic society now has a crucial role in analysing how these businesses behave, and in criticising them and voicing concerns. Crouch points out that even if particular behaviour is legal at the time of an event, analysis of the activity and its impact in terms of agreed ethical standards can lead to modified or new legislation.

In conclusion, to answer our two initial broad questions of whether ethical business behaviour is important and valid as an area of study, I have shown that the answer to both questions is 'yes'. I have argued that the idea that making a profit is the only responsibility a business has to society, or that business rules do not need to take account of personal or social principles, is not correct. Importantly, I have argued that it is imperative for organisations to behave well for four overlapping reasons – functional need, marketing need, regulatory need and moral imperative, and that these, together with related study of, and training in, business ethics, are all different manifestations of the same fact; that businesses are an integral part of society.

Finally, I would go further than saying that business ethics is important, and suggest that it is now essential, due to aspects of globalisation such as social media and other forms of information-sharing and consumer power that have greatly increased social and business interconnectedness, and that therefore organisations who want to operate successfully in today's global marketplace both need and are obliged to uphold and display ethical behaviour. It is true that there will be instances of businesses claiming to behave well that are not, but again, the increased exposure that social media and globalisation bring will arguably mean that organisations are not able to maintain such cover-ups on a large scale in the long term. This idea of increased interdependence due to globalisation is supported by Djelic and Etchanchu (2017), who show firstly that business, economics and politics have always been intertwined, and secondly that globalisation has magnified and deepened this connection. Thus I would suggest that the views of those such as Carr, Friedman and Wolf are doubly wrong, because not only have businesses always been part of society and therefore beholden to play by its rules, but that all parts of society are now even more interconnected in today's technological world.

References

Body Shop, The (2018) Modern Slavery Statement 2016/17, https://www.thebodyshop.com/en-gb/about-us/our-commitment/modern-slavery [Accessed 2/4/2018].

Bowie, N. E. (2017) *Business Ethics: A Kantian Perspective*. Cambridge: Cambridge University Press.

Carr, A. Z. (1968) 'Is business bluffing ethical?', *Harvard Business Review* 46(1), pp. 143–153.

Collins, J.W. (1994) 'Is business ethics an oxymoron?', *Business Horizons* 37(5), pp. 1–8.

Crane, A. and Matten, D. (2016) *Business Ethics* (4th edn). New York: Oxford University Press.

Crouch, C. (2011) *The Strange Non-Death of Neoliberalism*. Cambridge: Polity Press.

Djelic, M and Etchanchu, H. (2017) 'Contextualizing corporate political responsibilities: neoliberal CSR in historical perspective', *Journal of Business Ethics* 142(4), pp. 641–661.

Esty, D.C. (2007) 'What stakeholders demand.' *Harvard Business Review* 85(10), pp.30–34.

Ethical Consumer Research Association and Triodos Bank (2017) *Ethical Consumer Markets Report 2017*, http://www.ethicalconsumer.org/researchhub/ukethicalmarket.aspx [Accessed 24/3/2018].

Ethisphere (2018) The 2018 World's Most Ethical Companies Honoree List, http://www.worldsmostethicalcompanies.com/honorees [Accessed 15/4/2018].

Ferrell, O.C., Fraedrich, J. and Ferrell, L. (2002) *Business Ethics: Ethical Decision Making and Cases.* Boston: Houghton Mifflin.

Fisher, C, and Lovell, A. (2003) *Business Ethics and Values.* Harlow, Essex: Pearson Education.

Fortune (2017) The Fortune 2017 Change the World List. http://fortune.com/change-the-world [Accessed 4/4/2018].

Fritzsche, D. J. (2005) *Business Ethics: A Global and Managerial Perspective* (2nd edn). Boston: McGraw-Hill Irwin.

Good Shopping Guide, The, http://www.thegoodshoppingguide.com [Accessed 21/2/2018].

Green, R.M. (1994) *The Ethical Manager.* New York: Macmillan College Publishing.

International Organization for Standardization (ISO) (2010) *Guidance on Social Responsibility.* Geneva: ISO/TMBG Technical Management Board.

Prindl, R. and Prodham, B. (eds) (1994) *The ACT Guide to Ethical Conflicts in Finance.* Oxford: Association of Corporate Treasurers.

Ruggie, J. (2011) *Guiding Principles on Business and Human Rights: Implementing the United Nations "Protect, Respect and Remedy" Framework.* New York and Geneva: United Nations Human Rights.

Shaw, W.H. and Barry, V. (2007) *Moral Issues in Business* (10th edn). Belmont, CA: Wadsworth.

Svensson, G. and Wood, G. (2008) 'A model of business ethics', *Journal of Business Ethics 77*, pp. 303–322.

Trevino, L. K. and Nelson, K. (2010) *Managing Business Ethics* (5th edn). Hoboken, NJ: John Wiley.

UNFCCC (2015) *The roadmap for transforming the EU into a competitive, low-carbon economy by 2050.* https://ec.europa.eu/clima/sites/clima/files/2050_roadmap_en.pdf [Accessed 4/4/2018].

United Nations (2015) *Transforming our World: The 2030 Agenda for Sustainable Development*, https://sustainabledevelopment.un.org/post2015/transformingourworld [Accessed 4/4/2018].

US Senate Committee on Homeland Security (USS) (2011) *Wall Street and the Financial Crisis: Anatomy of a Financial Collapse.* Report by the Permanent Subcommittee of Investigations, April. Washington, DC: US Senate, https://www.hsgac.senate.gov/imo/media/doc/PSI%20REPORT%20-%20Wall%20Street%20&%20the%20Financial%20Crisis-Anatomy%20of%20a%20Financial%20Collapse%20(FINAL%205-10-11).pdf [Accessed 30/01/2018].

Wolf, M. (2000) 'Sleeping with the enemy', *Financial Times*, 16 May, p. 21.

Appendix 2

Answers to Over to You activities

Chapter A1

Over to You 1

The article is mainly a primary source for the authors' study and related data.
The sections in which the article is acting as a secondary source of other studies are:

'…the only similarly conducted study performed until now in young adults[38] revealed no effects of exercise level on the reasons for using DS'.

'This was in accordance with other qualitative[4] and quantitative studies.[18,19,22] Of those studies, only 9 papers were found that reported percentages of adolescents/young adults, who stated specific reasons for using DS.'

NB The numbers in subscript are numeric-style citations that refer to full references given at the end of the full article.

Over to You 2

1 Reliable information for general issues on disability but may be biased. Not an academic source.
2 Not reliable and not an academic source.
3 Reliable and an academic source, but 2011 is quite old for such a topic, which decreases how reliable the information will be.
4 Reliable for some ideas on issues, but may be biased and inaccurate. Not an academic source.
5 Reliable for introducing main issues, but not an academic source. Also the booklet is quite old for this topic, and this further decreases how reliable the source is for information on animal cloning.
6 Probably reliable as information from businesses, but not an academic source. You would also need to check when the website was updated.
7 Not reliable and not an academic source.
8 Reliable as information from businesses, but not an academic source.
9 Reliable for general discussion and ideas, but not peer-reviewed and therefore not academically reliable. You should find and use articles from the Centre's *Journal of Ethics* for academic sources.
10 Not reliable and will be biased, as it seems to be written by a pressure group. Not an academic source.

Chapter A3

Over to You 3

Carr assumes that businessmen are ethical in their private lives – this may not be true. He also assumes that all businesses operate in the same way, that they all have separate ethical standards from private ones, and that you always have to choose between losing and lying. This may not be true – there may be other options and other types of business model.

Carr also oversimplifies. He gives no evidence for his views and doesn't try to be objective or look at opposing evidence. His argument isn't very well ordered, as it is continuous opinion rather than a developed argument. I agree with Carr that some people feel they do need to lie in business, but not that this is always the case or that business ethics are totally separate from social norms – not true nowadays?

Carr's article seems to have been radical and important at the time (1968) because a lot of other texts still refer to it. In terms of business ethics he is definitely in the 'no' camp. His article is very dated now and things have moved on since then – now there is more legislation on regulation of corporate behaviour, corporate transparency and accountability, and more emphasis on ethics and sustainability.

Over to You 4

A Descriptive. The student introduces their own point in the first sentence, which is good, but from then on just reports what the source says without any comments or explanation of how it supports or does not support their own point. The student then moves on to a different point.

B Critical. The student introduces their own point, and then states that recent research supports their point and uses the sources as an example of this. They comment on what they see as a flaw in the research, but also comment on what they see as its value. Rather than then just moving on to a different point, they start to introduce further evidence to support their point.

C Descriptive. The student introduces their own point in the first sentence, which is good, but from then on just reports what the source says without any comments or explanation of how it supports or does not support their own point. The student then moves on to a different point.

D Critical. The student introduces their own point, and then states that recent research supports their point and uses the sources as an example of this. They comment on what they see as a flaw in the research, but also comment on what they see as its value. Rather than then just moving on to a different point, they start to introduce further evidence to support their point.

Chapter A4

Over to You 5

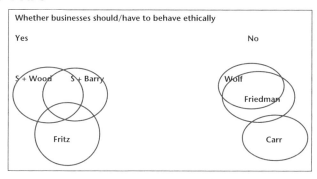

Chapter A5

Over to You 6

My comments	Carr, A. Z. (1968) 'Is business bluffing ethical?' *Harvard Business Review*, 46(1), pp. 143–153. Notes written on 3/3/2018
p. 145. Main point.	Ethics of bus. are diff. from 'civilised human relationships'. Uses poke analogy – needs 'distrust'.
p. 145. A generalisation and also I think much less true nowadays. 'somewhat diff.' means no rules?!	Most bus. people are ethical in private lives, but at work not 'private citizens' + follow 'somewhat different' rules.
p. 148 A good point! Probably true but hard to accurately evidence. Still, I think we should count good behaviour as ethical, even if done for cynical reasons	The image that bus. gives of using ethics is only a 'self-serving' + profit-making deception, not a true ethical position.
p.153. (Conclusion) Not true now/all businesses? bluffing = lying	'To be a winner, a man must play to win.' Busmn. will sometimes have to choose betwn. losing and bluffing (CP). To succeed he will have to 'bluff hard'.
Concl.	If buss. don't lie they won't grow and make profit.

Chapter B1

Over to You 7

1　This quotation is not special in what it says or how it is expressed. The student should have given this information in their own words as far as possible, e.g. Kzanty (2004) states that organs such as the lungs, pancreas and heart are used in transplantation.

2　This information is common fact and knowledge, so can be given in the essay without attribution to the author.

3　The quotation partially contradicts the student's point that transplants save lives.

4　The quotation is about the student's first point (improvements in transplantation techniques using animal organs), not about the point that is immediately in front of the quotation, that patients do not have to wait for transplants.

5　The quotation is not introduced clearly – it does not explain which trial or study is referred to or who 'everyone' is.

Over to You 8

1　There are no quotation marks and no in-text reference. This is plagiarism.

2　There is an in-essay reference but no quotation marks. This is plagiarism.

3　There are quotation marks but no in-text reference. This might be seen as plagiarism.

4　There are quotation marks and an in-text reference, but the authors' names should not be in brackets and the page number is missing. The page number must be included for quotations if you use the author/date system of referencing.

Over to You 9

1　The student has added the word *business* to the original wording. She should either take this word out or put it in square brackets, e.g. [business].

2　The student has taken out the words *synonymous with* from the original text. She should use an ellipsis (three dots with a space in between each one) to show this, e.g. 'good ethics is . . . good management (p. 2)'.

3　The topic words *good ethics* are used twice, once in the introductory sentence and again in the quotation. They should be used in one or the other, but not both, e.g. 'This idea is expressed succinctly by Collins (1994) in his discussion of good ethics when he states that "[It] is synonymous with good management" (p. 2).'

4　The full stop at the end of the quotation is inside the quotation marks. It should come outside the quotation marks, after the page-number brackets.

Correct version of the extract using a numeric system of referencing

> My first proposition is that businesses actually need to behave in an ethical manner. This idea is expressed succinctly by Collins when he states that 'good ethics is synonymous with good management' (1).

> Works Cited
> J. W. Collins (1994) 'Is business ethics an oxymoron?' *Business Horizons* 37(5): 1–8.

Chapter B2

Over to You 10

1 The paraphrase itself is good, as it is written in the student's own words. However, there are no in-text references and so this counts as plagiarism.

2 The paraphrase is rewritten in the student's own words and has an initial in-text reference. However, there is no reference reminder phrase in the second sentence and so it is not clear whether this sentence is an idea from the student or from the source. This could be seen as plagiarism.

3 There is only one in-text reference, given at the end of the paragraph. It is therefore not clear whether the first sentence is the student's idea or an idea from the source – this could be seen as plagiarism. It is much better to integrate a reference into the first sentence of a paraphrase and then to use reference reminder phrases.

4 This paraphrase consists of one sentence copied from Cox and a second sentence copied from the Maier, Blakemore and Koivisto text. The sentences have been stitched together without the use of quotation marks and without adequate referencing. This is plagiarism.

Example of an acceptable paraphrase of the Cox extract

Using the author/date style of in-text referencing:

> Cox (2003) suggests that advising caution in the use of mobile phones is an example of a typical approach to the fear of a possible health risk which may be of a serious nature. He states that such an approach may have negative consequences, but is taken because although there may in fact be no health risk, this has not yet been proven.

Using the number/footnote style of in-text referencing:

> Cox (1) suggests that advising caution in the use of mobile phones is an example of a typical approach to the fear of a possible health risk which may be of a serious nature. He states that such an approach may have negative consequences, but is taken because although there may in fact be no health risk, this has not yet been proven.

> Works Cited
> Cox, D. R. (2003) 'Communication of risk: health hazards from mobile phones', *Journal of the Royal Statistical Society: Series A* (Statistics in Society) 166(2), pp. 214–246.

Over to You 11

Example of an acceptable paraphrase

Using author/date in-text referencing:

> According to Meena et al. (2016), no direct evidence has been found to suggest a link between cancerous tumours (including brain tumours) and mobile phones, regardless of length of use.

Using numeric style in-text referencing (MLA):

> According to Meena et al. (1), no direct evidence has been found to suggest a link between cancerous tumours (including brain tumours) and mobile phones, regardless of length of use.

> Works Cited
> Meena, J. K., Verma, A., Kohli, C. and Ingle, G. K. (2016) 'Mobile Phone Use and Possible Cancer Risk: Current Perspectives in India', *Indian Journal of Occupational and Environmental Medicine* 20(1): 5–9.

Chapter B3

Over to You 13

Example of a one-sentence summary of the Dobson text

Dobson (2010) describes how the UK Department of Culture, Media and Sport supports all levels of sport but particularly sport for children, with the aim of encouraging life-long physical activity and good health.

Example of a two-sentence summary of the Dobson text

Dobson (2010) describes the main aims of the UK Department of Culture, Media and Sport as not only funding and supporting sport of all types and at all levels, but in particular, of increasing the amount of sporting opportunity and activity for school-age children. Dobson states that the DCMS hopes its specific targets in this area will lead to an improvement in the long term physical health of the UK population.

Chapter C1

Over to You 15

1 *Studying / examining / investigating* the possible . . . *Undergo* is only used for the people or things to which the experiment or event happen. For example: 'The patient will undergo two operations.' It is not used with *about*.

2 *Show / prove / illustrate*. It is already clear that cigarettes are harmful – the evidence is to show to what extent (how much) they damage health.

3 *Suggests / implies*. The word *impose* has a different meaning.

4   *states / suggests / shows* (other verbs are also possible). The verb *mention* is only used to refer to a minor point and therefore should not be used when summarising.

5   *Conceived.* This means when an idea is first thought of. *Perceived* means 'thought of / viewed in a particular way'.

6   *Invented. Established* means 'to set up something that continues', e.g. a company, charity or theory. *Discovered* would also be incorrect, as this verb can only be used when something is first found that already existed.

7   *Conveyed.* This means 'communicated'. *Portrayed* means 'represented or described in a particular way'.

8   The student has used the wrong verb (*implied*) to introduce the quotation. The quote from Murtaz is a clear statement, not something which he has only implied but not openly said. The student could have used a verb such as *stated, argued or asserted.*

9   The verb *claim* is often used to show that you do *not* agree with what the author says in the quotation. However, the student goes on to say that her essay will show that she thinks the statement in the quotation is correct. A more appropriate verb would have been a positive verb such as *show* or a more neutral verb such as *state* or *suggest.*

10   Discusses the portrayal . . . The verbs *discuss, describe* and *define* in the active voice are not followed by a preposition (e.g. *about / in / at / on*). They are followed by a noun only (e.g. 'I will discuss the issue' / 'Smith describes the effects').

Chapter C2

Over to You 16

1   There are several different <u>opinions / views / points of view</u> as to what constitutes an offence.

2   Brenner is a strong <u>advocate of</u> women's rights.

3   A primary <u>objection from</u> some religious groups to IVF is that it uses external fertilisation.

4   Balkin (2002) <u>opposes / is opposed to</u> sex segregation in schools in that it is a diversion from more important educative issues.

5   Many pressure groups have strong <u>views on</u> embryonic research.

6   Some people <u>take the view that</u> since they already pay income tax, they should not be additionally taxed on interest from savings.

7   This report has outlined the <u>arguments against / reasons for opposing</u> animal testing.

8   Mueller (2011) states that people often <u>reject</u> creative ideas because they are scared of change.

9   The current government in Mexico is adopting an expansionary economic <u>stance /</u>
    <u>position.</u>

10 A <u>counterargument </u>to humour being used to show dominance is that it is used to
    relieve social tension.

Chapter C3

Over to You 17

1   <u>In my view, / I suggest that</u> the issue of global warming is not as serious as the
    media portrays.

2   Kerlinger (1969) <u>states</u> that '*Science* is a misused and misunderstood word'
    (p. 1127).

3   It has been <u>claimed / suggested / stated / proven</u> that computer games can be
    used to educate children.

4   Smith (2009) has criticised Ramone's work <u>for</u> being overcomplicated.

5   Karl Marx <u>rejected</u> capitalism as a positive system for social development.

6   According to Gilchrist, we need to re-evaluate how we perceive risk-taking
    heroines, particularly those who are also mothers.

7   Kroll <u>uses // gives // quotes // paraphrases</u> Frie as an example of how early
    approaches to second-language learning saw teaching writing as secondary to
    speech.

8   The research team <u>acknowledges</u> that their data is incomplete and that further
    studies are needed.

9   According to <u>Reynolds (2000)</u> there is no strong evidence of long-term damage
    to health.

10 As Collins (1994) <u>states,</u> 'good ethics is synonymous with good management.' (p. 2).

Over to You 18

(Words given in Chapter C3 are underlined)
   There are three main and <u>distinct</u> theories of job satisfaction. One model states that
both job type and employee personality are central to determining job satisfaction.
This is because organisational structure influences the characteristics of a job, and jobs
with particular characteristics attract people with particular personality attributes.
These attributes in turn affect how satisfied a person will be with their job (Oldham
and Hackman, 1981). <u>In contrast</u> to this model, the dispositional approach sees a
person's disposition (or personality) as the most important element in determining
the level of job satisfaction, regardless of job type (Staw, Bell and Clausen, 1986).
Finally, Locke's theory of job satisfaction <u>differs from</u> both of the above, as it regards
what a person wants to do in a job and how far these goals are achieved as the main
factors that determine job satisfaction (Locke, 1968).

Chapter C4

Over to You 19

1   The new company is extremely <u>innovative</u>.

2   The National Bureau of Economic Research has been <u>of great benefit to</u> the field of economics in recent years.

3   I will look at both the theoretical and <u>substantive</u> implications of recent research on the consequences of job insecurity.

4   Lupton (1998) <u>claims</u> that the public is interested in health news. However, I will argue that media coverage in this area does not necessarily indicate genuine public interest.

5   Oswald's research <u>supports</u> the idea that having a job is more significant for happiness than being wealthy.

6   Jack, James and Roger's explanation of the effect of caffeine on performance seems to me the most <u>plausible</u> because . . .

7   The <u>validity</u> of this belief is called into question by recent evidence.

8   Although the survey is <u>extensive / wide-ranging</u>, it fails to look at applications of learning curve theory.

9   Carr (1968) uses the <u>illuminating</u> analogy of a poker player to demonstrate his position on business ethics.

10 Importantly, the findings are <u>consistent with</u> those of previous studies.

Chapter C5

Over to You 20

1   To state that cancer is caused by obesity is an <u>oversimplification.</u>

2   The study <u>claimed / maintained / asserted / suggested</u> . . . that mass media can be used to educate children but this was not borne out by the evidence.

3   The conclusion is <u>contradicted by</u> the data given earlier in the paper.

4   Tanen (2000) <u>claimed / maintained / contended / asserted (stated)</u> that visual imprinting occurs in infancy. However, this was shown to be incorrect by later studies.

5   Bijal (2002) <u>fails to consider</u> the fact that in most urban areas rich and poor sometimes live in close proximity.

6   Smith's study is <u>limited</u> because the sample size is extremely small.

7   The experiment was conducted according to a <u>standard / precise</u> method in order to ensure reliability.

8   The arguments in Bazer's article have a strong Eurocentric <u>bias / are highly biased towards</u> Europe.

9   Hooper's theory of the origin of the HIV virus <u>suffers from </u>lack of evidence.

10   The theory was <u>discredited</u> in 2001, when it was shown that there was no evidence to support it.

Over to You 21

Formal essay paragraph written from the informal critical analysis of the Carr article. (Underlined words are presented in the example sentences in Chapter C5.)

> Although Carr's argument may <u>seem</u> persuasive, <u>it has several flaws</u>. His <u>view lacks evidence</u> and he <u>does not take into account the fact that</u> business decisions are not always as clear cut as he suggests. He also <u>fails to consider</u> other potential business models and practices and <u>ignores the fact that</u> total separation of business from society is not possible.

Chapter D1

Over to You 23

Suggested answers (other alternatives are possible):

1   . . . detrimental to / has negative effects on . . . (avoid using *really* and *good* and *bad*)

2   . . . and this should not be allowed to continue.

3   The issue will be resolved / solved / dealt with . . .

4   There is no evidence that . . .

5   The fundamental issue is whether you have the ability to regulate your emotions.

6   Evidence such as . . . shows that companies need to …

7   It will not help us. / It will not solve the problem / situation.

8   There are different kinds of businesses such as private, public and non-profit making.

9   It's a serious / significant problem.

10   The most important action / step to take is to . . .

Over to You 24

Côté and Morgan demonstrated that as they predicted, suppressing unpleasant emotions leads to a decrease in job satisfaction and so an increase in intention to quit. Their findings also suggest that an increase in pleasant emotions will increase job satisfaction because it increases positive social interaction and responses from colleagues and customers.

Over to You 25

General comments: do not use general categories such as *women, men, people, everyone, we all, the politicians* and *in the modern world* because it is rarely the case that something applies to everyone or that we all know or think the same way. Always qualify your statements and make them as specific as possible, for example by using phrases such as *some women, the majority of manual workers . . . compared to western countries, many UK liberal politicians* and *most people are aware that . . .* As examples of this, below are suggestions for making sentences 1–7 more specific and supported:

1 The average income is significantly lower in countries that also have lower GDPs, and people in the lowest income brackets are usually in extreme relative poverty. For example, …

2 Portable technology is now used by the majority of consumers in developed countries.

3 Most people commonly think of writing as . . .

4 It is well established that drugs such as heroin, cocaine and cannabis and alcohol can often be addictive.

5 . . . . the majority of UK politicians across all parties disagree with this.

6 In North America, most of northern Europe, South Africa and some parts of Australia, abortion is either legal on request or legal if the mother's physical or mental health is deemed to be in danger (UN 2016).

7 There is evidence to suggest that in many Canadian cities, the majority of Chinese men in their twenties gamble to some extent. A study conducted by Papineau in 2005 showed that . . .'

Over to You 26

1 The pollution in the Mediterranean, which is the dirtiest sea in the world, is caused by tourism.

2 I have chosen to discuss cloning because I want to discuss the major advances in this technology and why cloning should be prohibited.

3 The issue of cloning animals and possibly humans has been debated by scientists, politicians and the general public.

4 The nephron has five main parts / components which / that are all essential for the process to work.

5 Academic writing is a form of writing that / which students need to adapt to and use in their work.

6 Personal writing is more concerned with personal feelings than with objective facts.

7 This is a development in the country's tourism industry.

8 Comment: *Vice versa* can only be used for a direct reversal of two things. In the student sentence it would mean that deoxygenated blood is also pumped from

the lungs into the heart. This is not correct, as only oxygenated blood flows back from the lungs to the heart. The sentence should therefore be, for example:

'Deoxygenated blood is pumped from the heart through the lungs and then the oxygenated blood flows back from the lungs into the heart.'

9 Comment: The use of the pronoun *they* means that the reader is not sure whether it is the children or the parents who behave aggressively. Also, the pronoun *them* could refer to films or to parents. If there is more than one subject in a sentence, use the full noun instead of a pronoun, or alter the sentence so that there is no other subject noun between the noun and the pronoun is refers to. For example: 'Luchens (2006) found that some children are allowed by their parents to watch violent films, and that these children behave more aggressively after watching such programmes.'
OR 'Luchens (2006) found that some parents allow their children to watch violent films and that they behave more aggressively after watching them.'

10 The government hopes that the legislation will protect the public so that a repetition of the level of fatalities that occurred between 1988 and 2001 can be avoided.

Chapter D2

Over to You 27

	Original extract	**Student paraphrase**
Order of information	1 Overlap but not equivalent	2 BE primarily concerned with issues not covered by law
	2 BE primarily concerned with issues not covered by law	1 Overlap but not equivalent
Synonyms	*not equivalent* *social rules* *primarily* *morally contestable*	*not synonymous* *acceptable behaviour* *mainly* *open to different* *interpretations*
Word form	*law* *regulations* *overlap (n)*	*legality* *regulates* *overlap (v.)*
Tense		No tense changes
Sentence structure		(Most sentence patterns and structures have been changed)

Over to You 28

A research study by Oswald (1997) challenges the common assumption that economic growth and increase in individual income in developed countries make people happier. He suggests that although many of us believe this to be the case, evidence shows that such increases in national wealth do not lead to any significant increase in how happy individuals feel.

Chapter D3

Over to You 29

1 According to Reynolds (2000), . . .

2 According to Padash (2000), . . .

3 Marchais (1984) discusses . . .

4 The year must be included and there should not be quotation marks around the authors' names.

5 Do not use bold, underline, italics or any other type of variant font for in-essay references (italics are sometimes used for a book/article titles).

6 The author and year should be used rather than the article title. If the article title is included it should be with initial capitals and either in quotation marks or in italics.

Over to You 30

1 Inadequate reference. The author (or organisation if no author) and year should be given, as with any reference. Words such as *article* or *book* should never be used as part of a bracketed reference.

2 You should not normally give the title of the book, and details such as edition numbers should not be used in an in-text reference (in fact *Economics* is only part of the book title; if you do want to include the title it must be accurate and in full). The correct reference should be (Sloman 1997).

3 Inadequate reference. If you want to include the title of an article or book you must also give the author and year: 'These factors are discussed by Smith (1990) in the article titled 'Biometric data of the future'.'

4 The author should be referred to, as with any other reference – not the website. For example, 'McDermot (1999) has drawn attention to the fact that more research needs to be done.'

5 Locke (1997) suggests that . . .

6 The in-text reference is missing.

Over to You 31

1 *In my view, . . .*   *According to* is only used when referring to other people. For example: 'According to Nitka (1980) . . .'

2 Kerlinger (1969) states that:

3 Jones (2002) demonstrates / shows that governments . . .   Don't mention details such as a book having been written or published.

4 As Collins (1994) states / suggests / claims . . .

5 These factors are discussed in the article 'Dying to be thin'.

6 The issue . . . is controversial.   Don't write about your reading / research process unless this is a specific part of the assignment.

Over to You 32

1 Côté and Morgan (2002) showed that . . .

2 Coates and Bailey (1995) examined . . .

3 According to the *New Scientist* (8 / 1 / 2005) people are still not . . .

4 As Crème and Lea (1997) have stated, the gap between . . .

5 Carr (1968) uses / gives the analogy of a poker game to explain his point.

6 According to Smith (2000), the problem is widespread.

Over to You 33

1 It is unclear where the quotation ends as there are three quotation marks. There is also an incorrect extra bracket at the end of the sentence.

2 The use of *which* introduces an 'extra information'/non-restrictive clause, but the end of the main clause is missing. The sentence therefore needs an ending such as the one suggested below (the main clause is in bold).

   The Body Shop, which for many years has branded itself as 'different because of our values' and which currently has an 'enrich not exploit' commitment policy (The Body Shop 2018), **is a leader in ethical sourcing**.

3 Knowles (1998) states that 'groups work more efficiently' (p. 64).

   NB This information is not special enough to use as a quotation and should have been paraphrased.

4 This quotation does not fit grammatically with the sentence and also contains information that is not special enough to quote. There should also be a bracket around the year of publication: Jones (2006) states that it is crucial that we understand the various causes of mental illness.

5 According to the *New Scientist* (8/1/2005), 'although we all use mobile phones, most of us still don't know about the possible physical or mental effects this use might have'.

6 As Trevino and Nelson (2010) state, 'Ethics is not just about the connection we have to other beings – we are all connected; rather, it's about the quality of that connection' (p. 32).

Chapter D4

Over to You 34

Sentences 1, 3 and 4 need a second clause.
  Suggested corrections:

1 Although there are several advantages, there are also drawbacks.

2 The theory cannot be viewed as valid, as they have found that it contains several inconsistencies.

3 As well as giving out benefits to families in poverty, the government needs a longer-term strategy.

Over to You 35

1 An increasing number of people **find it** difficult to get a job.

2 Guideline daily amounts on food labels **are** an alternative to . . .

3 . . . we still cannot assume that it really is **behaving** ethically.

4 The majority of drug users **are** aged between eighteen and thirty.

5 The study of business ethics **is** also important because it provides an informed framework.

Over to You 36

1 Côté and Morgan have shown that emotion regulation influences job satisfaction and that amplifying positive emotions increases positive interaction with both colleagues and customers. However, they have found that there is not an opposite correlation, that is, that job satisfaction affects emotion regulation.

2 The business decisions managers take can have significant implications, but/yet/ and most managers do not have training in business ethics. OR The business decisions managers take can have significant implications; however, / . However, most managers do not have training in business ethics.

3 The World Wide Web is a constantly developing technology and it has many advantages for society. OR The World Wide Web is a constantly developing technology; it has many advantages for society.

4 Lupton (1998) claims that the public is interested in health news; however, / . However, I will argue that media coverage does not indicate genuine public interest.

5 Wolf (2008) argues that business should not concern itself with social consequences; on the other hand, /. On the other hand, Svensson and Wood claim that business and society are co-dependent.

Over to You 37

Suggested improvements:

1 Collins (1994) suggests that if businesses do not operate with a degree of trust and co-operation inside the organisation, they will put constraints on profitability.

2 What the 2017 World Happiness Report suggests is that people need to feel that they have social support, the ability to make choices, and (that they) can trust national institutions.

3 Our survey revealed that students generally find understanding journal articles more difficult than listening to lectures.

4 Skrzypiec (2017) uses the ITT model to test how important taking drugs, fighting and stealing are as factors in adolescents' intention to transgress.

5 Having good neighbours, social events and healthcare are all . . .

Over to You 38

1 Wolf (2008) shares this view and Prindle (2009) also suggests that . . .

2 The solution was put into the test tube and was heated to 90 degrees.

3 If this theory were correct, it would mean that all previous data . . .

4 Ariti et al. (2018) have argued that farmer participation increases ownership and they have also suggested / also suggest that it helps social cohesion.

5 Geizen (2012) states that it is important to keep a megaproject as simple as possible.

Over to You 39

Suggested improvements:

1 According to Giezen's model, the probability of budget overrun in a megaproject can often be reduced by keeping it/the project as simple as possible (Giezen, M., 2012).

2 Team coaches were classified according to sport, and players according to both sport and the number of games they currently played each season.

3 The most important thing to consider at this meeting is the city's transport policy, as it will lead to an increase in traffic to the detriment of local air quality and noise pollution.

4 If these personal road accident stories are shared, such incidents (accidents) will hopefully be reduced.

5 The 2018 report is a key document showing the importance of job satisfaction, and both businesses and governments need to take this report seriously.

Over to You 40

1 Smith et al. (2000) report that this level of violence is harmful.

2 Recent research also shows that the drugs are effective.

3 Malicious software such as worms has been increasingly used.

4 The two types differ in the way they can be treated.

5 A research company has recently produced a new report.

Over to You 41

1 Marx argued for fundamental changes in society.

2 It is expected that the public will benefit from this technology.

3 The third disadvantage is that it is expensive.

4 For the/a majority of people, mobile phones are now almost indispensable.

5 The study shows that the immune system is extremely complex.

Over to You 42

1 Patel states that we developed music before language (Patel 2000, cited in Bragg 2003).

2 Prevention of type one diabetes is not possible.

3 They are both in a constant state of balance.

4 The negative effects of using genetically modified crops are listed below.

5 The materials used were pertinent to the experiment.

Over to You 43

1 capable of making

2 causes the temperature to rise

3 We discussed increasing

4 The failure of cells to remove

5 rejects the idea of using DNA

Over to You 44

1 The consultation process should continue to the final stage of the project.

2 The 2018 report will make an important contribution to the government's strategy.

3 The article clearly states that more research needs to be conducted.

4 To conclude / In conclusion, this essay has shown that . . .

5 There is still a potential market for buy to let construction developments.

Over to You 45

1 It has been shown in this essay that this is not the case.

2 It is illogical that people think pollution is not important.

3 The fact is that we cannot determine the outcome.

4 This essay will discuss the most important aspect of genetic research, that is, cloning.

5 Lenin (1914) claimed that a nation could not be truly free while it oppressed other nations.

Over to You 46

1 The study relevant to the debate is the one which is presented / that is presented / presented in Jacobs's 2017 paper.

2 The patients in the survey who / that experienced side-effects were taken out of the trial.

3 The company director who / that oversaw the project has written a book about her experience.

4 Out of the range of options many commentators have suggested the system which / that allows different states to have autonomy would be best.

5 The factors which / that might affect the way a text is written are listed below.

Over to You 47

1 The article summarised above, which contradicts my own data, has not been peer reviewed.

2 Social media, which is now a common publishing platform, challenges the concept of 'facts'.

3 Jacobs's data, which is summarised below in Figure 3, is . . . (OR, as a reduced clause) Jacob's data, summarised below in Figure 3, is . . .

4 (Same answer as for number 3 above)

5 Stockieve's theory has been used to justify violence, which was not his intention.
 NB Answer 5 is an example of *which* used to refer to the whole of the previous clause.

Over to You 48

1 Some theologians think that therapeutic cloning is acceptable.

2 Greenpeace states that one of its aims is to expose threats to the environment.

3 A country's government usually resides in the capital city.

4 An employee's career path is influenced by many different factors.

5 We analysed the students' questionnaires using this university's own software programme.

Over to You 49

1 The question is whether mobile phones make us sick.

2 The issue is whether this will lead to an increase in violence.

3 Research was conducted to see what the cause of the disease was.

4 We have not identified the problem with the strategy. / It is unclear what the problem with the strategy is.

5 The question remains as to what this research has achieved.

Appendix 3

Definitions of terms used in this book

abstract – the brief summary of an academic journal article, written by the author(s).

academic/scholarly journal – a journal that contains reliable, peer-reviewed articles.

academic source – a book, article or other type of text that has been peer reviewed and/or is written by experts in the subject.

analyse – to break down and examine something in detail, in order to then explain and evaluate it.

argument – a sequence of reasons to support a particular theory, proposition or point of view.

article – in an academic context, a self-contained piece of writing (often in the form of an essay) usually published in an academic journal.

NB Other meanings of *article* are a newspaper or magazine article, a piece of clothing, and the grammatical term for *a, an* and *the*.

bibliographic details – the full publication details of a source, given at the end of a written text.

citation – information on who wrote something, given within the piece of writing. *Citation* is also sometimes used to mean a quotation.

close paraphrase – when most of the words of the original source are used with only small changes.

critical reading and thinking – the process of identifying the argument of a text, analysing and questioning what it says, and then evaluating its strengths and weaknesses, relevance, importance and implications.

e.g. – abbreviation of the Latin *exempli gratia*, meaning 'for example'. Note that writing *e.g.* as *eg* (without a full stop after each letter) is becoming acceptable. Note also that *e.g.* and *i.e.* have different meanings (see *i.e.* below).

et al. – abbreviation of the Latin *et alii*, meaning 'and others'. Used for in-text referencing when a source has three or more authors.

evaluation/to evaluate – to reflect on and assess the value, merits, importance and implications of something.

extract (n.) – a section of text. This meaning is different from the verb *to extract*.

ibid. – from the Latin *ibidem*, meaning 'in the same place'. Used as an in-text reference to indicate that the source is exactly the same as the one previously given.

i.e. – from the Latin *id est*, meaning 'that is'. In writing *i.e.* is used to mean 'that is to say' or 'in other words'. When using *i.e.* you must give the complete idea or complete set of items, not just one or two examples. Compare with *e.g.* above.

insight – a new and/or deeper understanding about something.

journal – in an academic context, a journal is an academic (usually peer-reviewed) publication, usually published in several volumes each year.

NB *Journal* can also mean diary, newspaper or magazine.

literature – in an academic context, 'the literature' refers to scholarly publications in the field, i.e. books and academic articles that have been published in peer-reviewed journals.
NB This meaning is different from the more general use of *literature* to refer to novels and poems.

literature review – a summary of the key research relevant to a particular topic or issue, in order to give the research background and current context.

literature search – the process of looking for, finding and selecting relevant sources.

paraphrase / to paraphrase – re-expressing all the information and ideas from a section of text in one's own words and style.

peer review – the system by which articles are checked for quality and accuracy by relevant academic experts before being published.

perspective – in an academic context, a way of thinking about something; a particular point of view.

plagiarism / to plagiarise – presenting someone else's ideas, information, wording or style (or any combination of these) as one's own. Plagiarism also includes claiming that work done jointly with other students is solely one's own (this is called collusion). Plagiarism can occur accidentally due to poor writing and referencing practices or be committed on purpose.

primary source – the first, original source of information or idea. Examples are the original report written by the person who conducted an experiment, or the article or book where the author first presents their new idea, theory, argument or data.

quotation / to quote – a phrase, sentence or section of a source used in one's writing word for word, without any changes from the original.

reflective writing – a description of the writer's action, process or practice followed by a reflection in which the writer thinks about the motivations, strengths, weaknesses, significance and implications of their actions. The writer should also think about how the process has changed them or their views and what they might do differently in the future as a result. In an academic context, reflective writing often requires the writer to reflect on their actions in relation to theory and research in the field.

research – any type of organised search, study, investigation or work that is done in order to develop ideas and knowledge.

scan – to look at or read something quickly in order to identify key points and/or to assess whether something is relevant for more detailed reading.

school of thought – a way of thinking, set of beliefs, or accepted theory or approach, e.g. behaviourism, socialism, Marxism, feminism.

secondary source – a source which writes about, discusses or uses previously conveyed information and knowledge.

source – in an academic context, any type of material from which you get information (e.g. book, online article, website, video, newspaper).

synthesise (v.) synthesis (n.) – to compare and/or combine two or more things to create something new and/or more complex.

text – a general word used to describe any written document.
NB This is a different meaning from that of *to text* or a *textbook*.

Appendix 4

Dictionary use, register and word class

A dictionary word entry will give you information about the word's register, i.e. its style, context of use, and level of formality. If a word entry has one of the following labels next to it you should *not* use it in your essays: *inf.* (*informal*), *dated*, *archaic*, *poetic/literary*, *rare*, *humorous*, *euphemistic*, *dialect*, *offensive*, *vulgar*, *slang*, *derogatory*. Words that have no label or that are labelled as *formal* or *technical* are usually appropriate to use.

Use your dictionary to check:

● whether the word can be used as:
  a noun   e.g. **Consideration** of this issue is important.
  a verb   e.g. We need to **consider** this issue carefully.
  an adjective e.g. A **considerable** amount of research has been done on this issue.
  an adverb   e.g. We must conduct **considerably** more research on this issue.
  (See section on **word class** below.)

● if the word is a noun, whether it can be counted or is uncountable.
  For example, the word *consideration* can be counted:
      There **is** one key **consideration**. ✓
      There **are several considerations** to take into account. ✓

  But the word *research* cannot be counted:
      Important research has been conducted. ✓
      An important research has been conducted. ✗
      Several important **researches have been** conducted. ✗

● how the word fits into a sentence (its grammar). A good dictionary will give you example sentences for each word.

● whether the key word is often or always used with other specific words. This feature of language is called collocation. For example:
  Consideration **of** this issue is vital.
  This issue is currently **under** consideration by the government.
  Careful consideration of this issue is important.
  We need to **take into consideration** the long-term effects.

● whether the word has a positive or negative meaning (called connotation). For example, we don't say, 'There were abundant mistakes' because *abundant* has a positive meaning and is not used to describe something negative such as mistakes.

- common prefixes (such as *inter-* / *intra-* / *super-* / *anti-* / *poly-* / *post-* / *pre-*) which may help you understand the word, and what the correct negative form of the word is. For example, the negative form of *appropriate* is **in***appropriate*, not **un***appropriate*.

Using a thesaurus

A word entry in a thesaurus gives a group words with similar meanings (synonyms) but only in the very loosest sense, and often the words are not synonyms at all. For example, synonyms given for *analyse* in a thesaurus include *evaluate, interpret, judge* and *resolve*, none of which are precise equivalents; on the contrary, in academic study there are crucial differences in meaning between these words and *analyse*. It is not advisable to use a thesaurus to try to find synonyms in order to summarise or paraphrase.

Grammatical terms: word class

A dictionary entry will also give you information about the class of the word*, and it is therefore useful to have a basic understanding of these terms.

Adjective (adj.)

Adjectives describe a characteristic or quality of a noun. For example: 'It is an **arguable** issue.'
   Some adjectives have a comparative and a superlative form. For example: large, larger, largest.

Adverb (adv.)

Adverbs give more information about a verb, adjective or another adverb.
An **adverb** describing a *verb*: 'The economy *improved* **slowly**.'
An **adverb** describing an *adjective*: 'It is **arguably** an *important* issue.'
An **adverb** describing another **adverb**: 'We added the liquid **very carefully**.'

Article: The definite article is *a* or *an*, and the indefinite article is *the*.

Conjunction (conj.)

Conjunctions link clauses within a sentence or link separate sentences, showing the logical relationship between them. Coordinating conjunctions (*for, and, nor, but, or, yet, so*) link two independent clauses, and subordinating conjunctions (e.g. *after, although, even though, unless, whereas*) link a dependent clause to an independent one. Conjunctive adverbs (e.g. *accordingly, furthermore, however, nevertheless, moreover*) connect two separate sentences, and so need a semi-colon or full stop in front of them. Some conjunctions such as *after, before, as, since* and *until* can also be used as prepositions.

Demonstrative: *This, these, that* and *those.*

These can be used as pronouns (replacing the full noun). For example:
    There are three main **issues**. The most important of **these** is . . .
And they can be used as adjectives to help describe the full noun. For example:
    All of **these issues** are important.

Noun (n.)

A noun is a thing, place or person. Proper nouns are names of specific people or places, and abstract nouns (for example, *happiness* and *economics*) are nouns that represent a quality, state or idea. Some nouns are uncountable / mass nouns (for example *evidence, information* and *importance*) and are used in the singular form only. To talk about an uncountable noun in the plural you need to add another noun that indicates the plural aspect.

For example:

evidence:	the evidence**s** are ✗	the different type**s** of evidence ✓
information:	several information**s** ✗	several piece**s** of information ✓

Preposition (prep.)

Prepositions describe the time or space relationship between things.

Examples of prepositions are *in, at, on, of, to, with, over, under, between, through, during, before, after*.

Pronoun (pron.)

Pronouns replace full nouns.

The subject pronouns are *I, you, he, she, it, we* and *they*. For example:
    The diagrams in the text distract the reader from the main argument and **they** also overcomplicate the issue.

The object pronouns are *me, you, him, her, it, us* and *them*. For example:
    Our results indicate that job satisfaction is less important for new employees. **It** also seems to be less important for part-time employees.

The possessive pronouns are *mine, yours, his, hers, its, ours* and *theirs* and *whose*. For example:
    This book is *mine.*

The reflexive pronouns are *myself, yourself, himself, herself, itself, oneself, ourselves, yourselves,* and *themselves*. For example:
    Virginia Woolf thought of **herself** as a writer from an early age.

Quantifier

These are words such as *all, some, each, every, few, several, many* and *most*.

Verb (v.)

A verb represents an action, event or state. The verbs *be, do* and *have* can be used on their own as a main verb, or as a supporting (auxiliary) verb together with a main verb. As supporting verbs, *be, do* and *have* indicate either time, a negative or a question.

be, do, have as a **main verb**	**be, do, have** as a supporting/auxiliary verb + *main verb*
I **am** happy. I **was** happy	I **am** *studying* journalism
I **do** the same thing every day.	**Do** you **want** the job? I **don't** *want* the job.
I **have** a car.	I **haven't** *seen* the film.

The verbs *will, shall, can, could, may, might, must, should, ought to* and *would* (and the phrases *to be able to, to need to* and *to have to*) can only be used as supporting, auxiliary verbs to express possibility, request, necessity, certainty or caution. These verbs are called modal or modal auxiliary verbs. They are called modal verbs because they indicate the 'mood' of the main verb.

Modal verb + *main verb*

We **should** *consider* all aspects of the issue. The data suggest that there **might** *be* a link.

*Note that many words can belong to more than one word class depending on how they are used. For example:

The government will **debate** the motion next week.	*Debate* used as a verb.
There has been a great deal of **debate** on the ethics of cloning.	*Debate* used as a noun.

Appendix 5

Referencing styles

Below is a brief overview of the five main referencing styles. Different universities and faculties within them may have their own variations of these styles, particularly in the way page numbers are indicated, how brackets are used, and whether book/journal titles are underlined, italicised or put in bold. Practice also varies as to whether the list of sources at the end of an essay is called a Reference List or a Bibliography.

Don't worry too much about such variations when you start your course; your tutors will not expect you to get every detail of referencing correct at first. The most important thing is to indicate clearly in your essay (not just in your list of references) whenever you have used a source, even if you make small mistakes in how you do it. Always check and use the referencing guide given to you for your course, and try to be consistent in the way you reference.

1 Harvard referencing

This is an author and date (year) system used in many disciplines.

In your essay

Quotation

Collins (1994: 2) states that 'good ethics is synonymous with good management'.
or
Collins (1994) states that 'good ethics is synonymous with good management' (p. 2).
or
I will argue that 'good ethics is synonymous with good management' (Collins 1994 p. 2).

Paraphrase

Collins (1994) believes that you cannot manage well without having good business ethics.
or
One view is that you cannot manage well without having good business ethics (Collins 1994).

In your list of references*

(References should be listed in alphabetical order of author's family name):
Collins, J.W. 1994 'Is business ethics an oxymoron?' Business Horizons Vol. 37(5), pp. 1–8.

2 American Psychological Association (APA) referencing

This is an author and date (year) system used in the social sciences. There are some small differences between the APA and Harvard system.

In your essay

Quotation

Collins (1994) states that 'good ethics is synonymous with good management' (p. 2).

Paraphrase

Collins (1994) believes that you cannot manage well without having good business ethics.

In your list of references

Collins, J.W. (1994) 'Is business ethics an oxymoron?' *Business Horizons* 37(5), pp. 1–8.

3 Modern Language Association (MLA) referencing

This is an author and page system used in the humanities and liberal arts.

In your essay

Quotation

Collins states that 'good ethics is synonymous with good management' (2).

Paraphrase

Collins (2) believes that you cannot manage well without having good business ethics.

In your list of references

Collins, John W. (1994) 'Is business ethics an oxymoron?' *Business Horizons* 37(5):1–8.

---

* The terms 'references' and 'bibliography' are sometimes used interchangeably, but strictly speaking a bibliography differs from a list of references because it contains all sources read, including those not cited explicitly in the essay.

4 Numeric style British Standard

This is a numeric system.

In your essay

Quotation

Collins [1] states that 'good ethics is synonymous with good management'.

Paraphrase

Collins [1] believes that you can't manage well without having good business ethics.

In your list of references

(References are listed in numerical order, not alphabetical order.)
1. Collins J W. Is business ethics an oxymoron? *Business Horizons*, 1994, 37(5)1–8.

5 Vancouver referencing

This is a numeric system often used in field of medicine. There are several small variations within this system so check your course referencing guidelines.

In your essay

Quotation

Collins [1] states that 'good ethics is synonymous with good management'.
or
Collins[1] states that 'good ethics is synonymous with good management'.

Paraphrase

Collins [1] believes that you can't manage well without having good business ethics.
or
Collins[1] believes that you can't manage well without having good business ethics.

In your list of references

(References are listed in numerical order, not alphabetical order.)
1. Collins J W. Is business ethics an oxymoron? *Business Horizons* 1994; 37(5):1–8.

6 Chicago/Turabian referencing

This is a numeric system.

In your essay

Collins[1] states that 'good ethics is synonymous with good management'.

In your footnotes

1. John W. Collins, 'Is business ethics an oxymoron?' *Business Horizons* (1994): 37(5), pp. 1–8.

Vocabulary index

Bold page numbers indicate a word definition (the word will also be found in an example sentence in the relevant section).
Unbold page numbers indicate where an undefined word can be found in an example sentence.

Subject index